Documents and Debates
General Editor: John Wroughton M.A., F

# Seventeenth-Century Europe

## Gary Martin Best M.A.

Head of History, Newcastle-under-Lyme School

Macmillan Education

First published 1982

Published by
MACMILLAN EDUCATION LIMITED
Houndmills Basingstoke Hampshire RG21 2XS
and London
Associated companies throughout the world

Printed in Hong Kong

*British Library Cataloguing in Publication Data*

Seventeenth century Europe. — (Documents and
 debates)
 1. Europe — History
 I. Best, Gary Martin  II. Series
 940.2'5      D273

 ISBN 0−333−31222−8

# Contents

# Acknowledgements

The author and publishers wish to thank the following who have kindly given permission for the use of copyright material:

George Allen & Unwin (Publishers) Ltd for an extract from *Richelieu and His Age* by C T Burckhardt;

Edward Arnold (Publishers) Ltd for extracts from *Germany in the Thirty Years War* translated by G Benecke, and *Sweden as a Great Power 1611–97* translated by M Roberts, from the Documents of Modern History series, and The '*Thirty Years War' and the Conflict for European Hegemony 1600–1660* by S H Steinberg, from the Foundations of Modern History series;

B T Batsford Ltd for an extract from *The Thirty Years War* by J V Polisensky;

John Calder (Publishers) Ltd for extracts from *Simplicius Simplicissimus* by H J C von Grimmelshausen, translated by H Weissenborn and L Macdonald;

Cambridge University Press for an extract from *The Revolt of the Catalans* by J H Elliott;

Jonathan Cape Ltd for an extract from *The Thirty Years War* by C V Wedgwood;

Constable & Co. Ltd for extracts from *The First Bourbon* by Desmond Seward and *Madame de Maintenon* by Charlotte Haldane;

J M Dent & Sons Ltd for extracts from *The Age of Louis XIV* by Voltaire, translated by M P Pollack (Everyman's Library series);

Hamish Hamilton Ltd for extracts from *Historical Memoirs of the Duc de Saint-Simon*, Volumes 1–3, translated by Lucy Norton;

D C Heath and Company for an extract from *Problems in European Civilization: Peter The Great, Reformer or Revolutionary?* translated by Marc Raeff;

The Historical Association for an extract from *History*, 1947;

Longman Group Limited for an extract from *Louis XIV* translated by H G Judge;

W W Norton & Company Inc. for extracts from *Louis XIV* by J B Wolf;

Oxford University Press for extracts from *Sir William Temple's Observations upon the United Provinces of the Netherlands* edited by Sir George Clark, and from *A Supplement to Burnet's History of My Own Time* edited by H C Foxcroft;

Princeton University Press for extracts from *Czechoslovakia in European History* by S Harrison, 2nd revised edition, Copyright 1943, 1953 by Princeton University Press, and from *Richelieu and Reason of State* by William F Church, Copyright 1972 by Princeton University Press;

Routledge & Kegan Paul Ltd for extracts from *The Private Life of the Marshal Duke of Richelieu* translated by F S Flint, and from *The General Crisis of the Seventeenth Century* by G Parker and L M Smith;

Thames and Hudson Ltd for an extract from *Peter the Great* by M S Anderson;

Walker and Company, New York, for extracts from *War, Diplomacy, and Imperialism 1618–1768* edited by Geoffrey Symcox. Copyright © 1974 by Geoffrey Symcox; from *The Low Countries in Early Modern Times* edited by Herbert H Rowen. Copyright © 1972 by Herbert H Rowen, and from *The Century of Louis XIV* edited by Orest and Patricia Ranum;

Weidenfeld (Publishers) Limited for extracts from *The Golden Century* by Maurice Ashley, and *Essays in Swedish History* by Michael Roberts.

Every effort has been made to trace all the copyright holders but if any have been inadvertently overlooked the publishers will be pleased to make the necessary arrangement at the first opportunity.

*Author's Acknowledgements*
I would like to thank the librarians in Bath Public Library, Bath Reference Library, and the Bodleian Library, Oxford for all their assistance. I would also like to thank my wife for all the patience she showed in the preparation of this book, and acknowledge my debt to my mother, who first inspired me with a love of history.

# The Seventeenth Century

"Tis all in pieces, all coherence gone . . . new Philosophy calls all in doubt. . . . And freely men confess that this world's spent.' So wrote John Donne, expressing the deep sense of confusion that had arisen in men's thinking thanks to the uncertainty created by two centuries of dramatic change in every sphere – political, religious, economic, social, even cultural. Some historians have recently begun to argue that the seventeenth century was essentially a period which witnessed 'a struggle for stability', a search for new foundations on which to base society, and that the real 'crisis' was reached in the devastations of the Thirty Years War and the series of revolutions and rebellions which broke out in the 1640s and 1650s. Whether or not there was a 'general crisis' and, if so, what sort of crisis it was, is something that historians have hotly debated in recent years, and a section of this book has been devoted to it. Certainly both the mid-century civil unrest and the Thirty Years War contributed towards the development of the so-called 'age of absolutism', and a resulting degree of stability and assurance that had been lacking earlier. The civil unrest, though partly caused by assertive monarchies, clearly demonstrated the anarchy which could result from weak governments, while the Thirty Years War, the first conflict to be European in its scale, helped to produce what some have described as a 'military revolution', in which new standing armies, more professional and better disciplined, replaced the mercenaries of military entrepreneurs like Wallenstein and required higher revenues, which in turn necessitated economic growth and the formation of a royal bureaucracy.

Almost all seventeenth-century thinkers came to believe that the world in its ideal state was an orderly place governed by God-given laws, which were discoverable by human reason. It was man's unreasonable passions that created the world's problems, and, therefore, to control man's passions became what some historians have described as 'the central preoccupation of the age'. Hobbes argued that human passions made life 'solitary, poor, nasty, brutish and short', so that the sovereign power in the state should be 'great enough for our security'. If many did not accept his ideas, based as they were on political expediency, most were prepared to believe by the latter half of the seventeenth century that good government was achievable only through the absolutism of kings appointed by God to carry out his will through the maintenance of law.

Bossuet expressed the theory of divine right perfectly when he said: 'The royal throne is not that of a man, but the throne of God Himself . . . only God may judge over their judgements. . . . The whole state is in him.' Louis XIV, who embodied such kingship, commented on the relationship between king and country that 'the good of one constitutes the glory of the other'. That society was prepared to accept such claims is an indication of the importance of security because of the ever-present threat of foreign invasion and internal disunity. In Pufendorf's contemporary assessment of Europe, 'mightily disjoined' Spain (and hence its declining status) is contrasted with the strength of unified France 'swarming with people and sowed thick with cities and towns'. Sovereigns increasingly began to rely on intendants or commissioners, men appointed by them and therefore loyal to them, to create a more centralised nation–state. Statistical and other factual evidence increasingly became the basis for government policies. The historian Lossky has argued that 'the establishment of the principle of obedience to the lowly agent of the central power is the crucial theme in the emergence of the modern state. Everywhere in Europe this development took a long step forward during the seventeenth century.'

However, few sovereigns were revolutionary enough to attempt the destruction of the old systems of government and create a completely new state. The centralising tendencies of the emerging sovereign states heightened the class-consciousness of the aristocracy, many of whom saw themselves as the natural guardians of the state, inheriting from their ancestors special gifts for leadership. Though they disliked men recently ennobled, they were prepared to unite with them in defence of local institutions and customs. It would be wrong to apply modern notions of 'privileged' and 'unprivileged' to the seventeenth century, for every individual and every group possessed its 'liberties', its privileges and special rights, and nearly all rebellions were sparked off by real or imaginary grievances at innovations from above that seemed to threaten the status quo. In many cases, such as that of the boyars in Russia, the nobles did not accept the increasing power of the sovereign until their own social privileges were confirmed and strengthened. Even Louis XIV dared not try removing the tax exemption of the rich. Many factors limited the effectiveness of so-called 'absolute' governments – and indeed of the increasing national awareness for, as Ranum says, 'regional particularism remained so strong that Frenchmen, Englishmen, and Spaniards did not have to cross the borders of their kingdoms in order to feel foreign and ill at ease among strange ways and beliefs'. Nevertheless, officeholders and nobles did become more orderly and obedient, and Rabb has recently argued that 'none of the troubles of the late seventeenth century, in contrast to their predecessors, seriously threatened or fundamentally questioned the entire system of government, the very organisation of politics. *That* was the crucial change. . . . This outcome, moreover, represented the conclusive establishment of the structure that is recognisable as the modern state, organised around an impersonal, centralised, and unifying system of government, resting on law, bureaucracy, and force. Since the mid-seventeenth-century upheavals proved to be the last major effort to resist the consolidation of that structure and to defend local autonomies, their failure marked a decisive change of direction in the development of Western society.'

Economic activity increased in the seventeenth century, but not at the rate it had in the previous century. Some have attributed this to the lack of a middle class. In most of Europe there was no identifiable middle-class group, merely town communities, each with its own professional corporations. Even in the Dutch Republic, the tone of social and political life was set by the regents and patricians who were not directly involved in trade. However, it would be wrong to assume only the middle class can be 'the architect of material well-being'. Other factors were involved. Though prices were fairly constant, there were important variations from region to region, created by a combination of natural factors, such as the climatic conditions, with artificial ones, such as the operation of tariffs, the sale of monopolies, and the debasement of coinage. Therefore manufacturers and merchants were reluctant to take chances, especially as their markets were restricted by the fundamentally agrarian nature of society. Nine-tenths of people worked on the land and most were hide-bound by tradition and seldom looked beyond the village in which they lived. No change could be expected there until their landlords desired it, and with the notable exception of Britain, such a desire was lacking, perhaps because 'the association of commercial farming with the stigma of the bourgeois worked against the practice of successful state management' (Maland). Unable to achieve greater productivity, most Europeans suffered from poor health and a low life expectancy – and they certainly did not have money to spend on manufactured goods.

However, many historians argue it would be wrong to think of the seventeenth century as a period of economic stagnation. Indeed, Marxist historians like Hobsbawm argue that changes between 1600 and 1700 amounted to a 'fundamental solution of the difficulties which had previously stood in the way of the triumph of capitalism', with the English Civil War marking a turning-point. Others reject this, but point out important changes. Two examples will suffice. The first is that this century saw the final stages of the long process by which the centre of trade moved from the Mediterranean to the Atlantic seaboard, to Britain, France, and, of course, the Dutch Republic, which experienced its 'golden age'. The second is the development of mercantilism. Economic as well as political unification was desirable because of the burden imposed on royal exchequers by warfare and bureaucracy. Most governments were chronically in debt – indeed, the century has been called 'the golden age for private enterprise in government finance'. Spain provides an obvious example with her repeated bankruptcies – by 1670, as a result of her impaired credit, she was paying 40 per cent interest on some of her loans. Not surprisingly, sovereigns became concerned to exploit natural resources for the acquisition of power. As Colbert remarked, 'Trade is the source of finance and finance is the vital nerve of war'. This approach was a far cry from the older view of men like Sully and Richelieu who regarded trade as something created by God to spread peace, unity, and the gospel. The later seventeenth century witnessed a new phenomenon — wars motivated solely for commercial ambitions.

Some historians see this period not so much as an age of crisis or consolidation as 'a golden age'. In part this stems from seeing the century as an era of increasing religious toleration. The Thirty Years War is alleged to have revealed the uselessness of force as a means of reconverting Europe to catholicism and therefore to have ended the era of religious wars. 'Men of different opinions worship God in their own way', wrote one contemporary Englishman. 'We are to respect them in their different manner of worship.' This 'calming-down' of religious attitudes was a significant change. No longer did the church, catholic or protestant, pursue extravagent witch-hunts or attack so fiercely new scientific developments. 'Religion', remarked Pascal, 'draws into a unity the scattered elements in our lives. It answers the questions which reason only can raise, and . . . it cannot be in opposition to reason or science because it includes yet transcends both.' However, sovereigns continued to dislike all signs of religious nonconformity within the state — as is so clearly seen in Louis XIV's action against the Huguenots or Leopold I's persecution of the Hungarians. The church was too vital an organisation to be left alone because it alone embraced the entire realm and yet penetrated to every district and village. Tolerance tended to be present only where economic or political circumstances made it useful — and even then some historians argue it tended to be toleration of protestant by protestant rather than between catholic and protestant.

Far safer are those arguments based on presenting the century as a golden age in the arts and sciences. Rubens and Velasquez, Shakespeare and Cervantes, Molière and Racine, Milton and Dryden — the list is endless. Voltaire remarked that the flowering of the arts amounted to 'a general revolution'. Even language itself developed with governments adopting their own national languages to replace Latin, though this created a linguistic distinction between classes and sometimes (notably in the Habsburg Empire) between dominant and subject peoples. The century also witnessed 'revolutionary progress in philosophic and scientific thought' (Ogg) for it was the era of Descartes, Spinoza, Leibniz, Huygens, Locke and Newton. As Ashley remarks, the seventeenth century 'was indeed, if not the apogee, certainly a high point of civilisation in which all Europeans have reason to glory'. One spin-off from this was that an increasingly large reading public was interested in reading about contemporary political, social, and cultural developments — and therefore sources for historians of the period are diverse: published diaries and memoirs, travel accounts and travel diaries, pamphlets and broadsheets, novels and letters, edicts and memoranda, etc. Hopefully the documents selected here will stimulate thought about how contemporaries viewed personalities and events as well as how historians view them. One thing is certain amid all the debates on the seventeenth century: it was an age not only of great events, but also of great personalities: great ministers like Richelieu and Olivares, great leaders like de Witt and Oxenstierna, and great monarchs like Gustavus Adolphus, Peter the Great, and Louis XIV. This 'age of courts and kings', as Erlanger calls it, will long continue to fascinate and attract those who turn to its study.

## Further Reading

The best introductions to the period are to be found in D. Maland, *Europe in the Seventeenth Century*, Macmillan, 1966; D. H. Pennington, *Seventeenth-Century Europe*, Longman, 1970; R. Hatton, *Europe in the age of Louis XIV*, Thames & Hudson, 1969; E. N. Williams, *Dictionary of English and European History 1485–1789*, Penguin, 1980; and E. N. Williams, *The Ancien Regime in Europe 1648–1789*, Bodley Head, 1970. Volumes in three series are well-worth reading: in the Fontana History of Europe, G. Parker, *Europe in Crisis 1598–1648* (1979) and J. Stoye, *Europe Unfolding 1648–88* (1969); in Harper & Row's The Rise of Modern Europe, C. J. Friedrich, *The Age of the Baroque 1610–60* (1952), F. L. Nussbaum, *The Triumph of Science and Reason 1660–85* (1953), and J. B. Wolf, *The Emergence of the Great Powers 1685–1715* (1951); and in The New Cambridge Modern History, vol IV, *The Decline of Spain and the Thirty Years War*, vol V, *The Ascendancy of France*, and vol VI, *The Rise of Great Britain and Russia*.

Other useful books on the period are: D. Ogg, *Europe in the Seventeenth Century*, A. & C. Black, 1960; L. Cowie, *Seventeenth-Century Europe*, Bell, 1960; M. Ashley, *The Golden Century*, Weidenfeld & Nicolson, 1969; and G. N. Clark, *The Seventeenth Century*, Oxford University Press, 1947. Interesting aspects of the century are dealt with in: V. L. Tapie, *The Age of Grandeur*, Weidenfeld & Nicolson, 1960; F. B. Artz, *From Renaissance to Romanticism*, Chicago, 1962; P. Hazard, *The European Mind 1680–1715*, Penguin, 1964; G. N. Clark, *War and Society in the Seventeenth Century*, Cambridge University Press, 1957; G. R. Cragg, *The Church and the Age of Reason 1648–1789*, Penguin, 1960; and T. K. Rabb, *The Struggle for Stability in Early Modern Europe*, Oxford University Press, 1975.

Useful extracts from the philosophers and writers of the century can be found in S. Hampshire, *The Age of Reason*, Mentor, 1955, and A. Lossky, *The Seventeenth Century*, The Free Press (Macmillan), 1967. An interesting selection of documents can be found in O. and P. Ranum, *The Century of Louis XIV*, Macmillan, 1972.

# I  The French Restoration of Royal Authority

## Introduction

Henry IV established a new dynasty dedicated to the restoration of royal authority after years of civil conflict. He recognised the need to conciliate the various factions within France, and this 'most French of French kings' had the extrovert character necessary to 'make conciliation appear a strong policy' (extract 1). His government was essentially a conservative one; there were no fundamental reforms and much depended on Henry's personality. The one major change was unintentionally created by Sully's introduction of the *paulette*. Some argue it provided the basis for absolutism, identifying the *officier* interests with those of the crown; others question how any monarchy could become absolute once it accepted an independent class and an inefficient financial system. His successors believed they owed a great debt to *Henri le Grand*, and many looked back to the reign of this 'earthy cynic who believed in authoritarian rule, but who understood people' (Brown) as a golden era (extract 2).

It was said that French kings 'can do what they will, but they need to will it strongly'. The minority of Louis XIII was therefore a dangerous interlude, but from it emerged the strong will of Cardinal Richelieu, 'the torment and ornament of the age'. He set France on the road to European hegemony, contributing the phrase *raison d'état* to the vocabulary of political thought (extract 3). Though he described himself as just the king's *créature*, most contemporaries believed he was the real power in France and many historians have belittled Louis XIII's contribution to government. The relationship between the two men is one of the most interesting aspects of the period (extract 4). The picture of Richelieu as a Machiavellian, coldblooded 'superman' is now being reviewed. Though some historians see the restoration of royal authority as a radical innovation in the light of the events of 1559–1630, in many respects Richelieu's government was a conservative one and, though he tackled the nobles and the Huguenots, he allowed new powerful groups, such as the financiers, to emerge. Some historians argue that 'this powerful regime contributed little except despotic energy to the problem of creating a centralised state'.

To contrast Mazarin with Richelieu was, and still is, a popular pursuit (extract 5). Mazarin's main interest was diplomacy and his success in that field is usually recognised, but to a large extent he remains an enigma and, apart from the period of the Fronde, his administration is only slightly researched. The Fronde has been described both as 'a crisis – economic, demographic, social, physiological, and moral – of an intensity and duration hitherto unknown' (Goubert) and as 'a period of imprudence and exaggeration lacking sense or aim' (Kossmann). Was it a protest of the old feudal aristocracy under political and economic pressure? A reaction by the new aristocracy to the move towards a centralised monarchy? An abortive liberal revolution of the people against a feudal state? A response to economic and demographic recession aggravated by the effects of a war? Or was it just a series of anarchical events provoked by an incompetent government and the self-interest of powerful individuals and groups? Many historians have distinguished between a Fronde of the Parlement (extract 6) and a Fronde of the Nobility (extract 7); others argue that both were part of a 'general crisis' affecting Europe (see section X). From the Fronde there emerged a much stronger monarchy. Though Mazarin, according to contemporaries, 'had no sufficient understanding of internal affairs', his government saw the theory of royal absolutism converted into a practical possibility by the development of a more systematic administration than France had ever had before: a paradox that has yet to be resolved.

## Further Reading

Excellent introductions to the period can be found in W. E. Brown, *The First Bourbon Century in France*, University of London, 1971; J. Lough, *An Introduction to Seventeenth-Century France*, Longman, 8th edn, 1969; A. Maurois, *A History of France*, Methuen, 1964; D. Sturdy, *Royal Authority in France: 1589–1643*, Gill and Macmillan, 1973; and G. R. R. Treasure, *Seventeenth-Century France*, Murray, 2nd edn, 1981.

For the reign of Henry IV, see D. Seward, *The First Bourbon*, Constable, 1971, and D. Buisseret, *Sully and the Growth of Centralised Government in France*, Eyre and Spottiswood, 1968. For the reign of Louis XIII and Richelieu, the best introduction is C. V. Wedgwood, *Richelieu and the French Monarchy*, English Universities Press, rev. edn, 1962. More detailed information can be found in C. J. Burckhardt, *Richelieu and His Age* (3 vols), Allen and Unwin, 1967, 1970, 1972; O. A. Ranum, *Richelieu and the Councillors of Louis XIII*, Oxford University Press, 1963; and G. R. R. Treasure, *Cardinal Richelieu and the Development of Absolutism*, A. and C. Black, 1972. There is no really good biography of Mazarin, though A. Hassall, *Mazarin*, London, 1903, is still useful. Two interesting (and different) views of the Fronde can be found in P. R. Doolin, *The Fronde*, Harvard University Press, 1935, and E. H. Kossmann, *La Fronde*, Leiden, 1954 (in French).

Those interested in looking at further documents and articles should see W. F. Church, *The Impact of Absolutism in France: National Experience under Richelieu, Mazarin, and Louis XIV*, John Wiley, New York, 1969, and J. H. Shennan, *Government and Society in France 1461–1661*, Allen & Unwin, 1969.

## 1   The Liberator and Restorer of the State

If I wanted to acquire the title of orator I would have learned some fine, long harangue and would have spoken it to you gravely enough. But, gentlemen, my desire is to attain to two more glorious titles, which are to call myself liberator and restorer of this State. For which end I have
5   summoned you. You know to your cost, as I do to mine, that when God called me to the Crown, I found France not only almost ruined, but almost entirely lost to Frenchmen. By the grace of God, by the prayers and by the good advice of those of my servants who do not follow the soldier's profession; by the sword of my brave and generous nobility,
10   among whom I do not take special account of princes, but only of our finest title, the honour of a nobleman; by my toils and troubles, I have preserved her from this fate. Together we must now save her from ruin. Share with me, my dear subjects, in this second glory, as you have already shared in the first. I have not summoned you as did my predecessors,
15   simply to approve their wishes. I have brought you together to hear your advice, to consider it, to follow it, in short to put myself in guardianship under your hands, an ambition which is not often found among kings who are greybeards and victorious. But the fierce love which I bear my subjects, the keen desire that I have to add those two fine titles to that of
20   King, makes it seem to me both pleasant and honourable.

H. de Beaumont de Péréfixe, *Histoire du Roy Henry le Grand*, trans. by J. Dauncey, *The History of Henry IV*, 1664, p 244

*Questions*

a   Henry IV later commented on this speech to the Assembly of Notables in 1597 that he had meant what he said, but 'I meant it with a sword by my side'. What does the speech (and the later comment) tell you about the aims, methods, and character of the king?

b   Compare this speech with extract 6(c). What are the apparent differences between them in their attitude towards the monarch's role?

\* c   Why was France 'almost ruined' and 'almost entirely lost to Frenchmen' (lines 6–7) when Henry ascended the throne?

\* d   Who were the men who gave Henry 'good advice' (lines 8–9)?

\* e   What issues had been involved in the civil war from which Henry emerged as king? Pascal once said, 'The greatest of all evils is civil war. The evil to be feared from a fool who succeeds by right of birth is not as considerable nor as certain.' Was this the only reason why Henry IV was able to win support as 'liberator and restorer' (line 4) of France?

## 2 The 'Chicken in the Pot' King

The picture I keep of things as they were in those days still fills me with happiness. I see again, with the keenest pleasure, the beauty of the countryside as it was then; it seems to me that meadows were greener than they are now, that trees bore more fruit. . . . Flocks were driven to the
5 fields in safety while the peasants ploughed the land to sow wheat which tax gatherers and soldiers never plundered. They had goods and possessions sufficient enough and slept in their own beds. When it came to harvest time how pleasant it was to see troops of reapers, each one stooped by the other, working the furrows and garnering bunches of corn which
10 the stronger tied for the rest to load as sheaves into the carts; afterwards children who had been watching the flocks far away were able to glean ears of corn which a feigned carelessness had left for them. . . . After the harvest the peasants chose a holiday when they could all meet. . . . They invited not just friends but their masters too and were overjoyed if these
15 took the trouble to come. . . .
  When our good people celebrated their children's marriages it was a delight to see how they dressed; for beside the bride's finery, never less than a red gown and a head-dress trimmed with tinsel and glass beads, the parents were clad in their own pleated blue dresses which they had taken
20 out from chests scented with lavender, dried roses and rosemary. . . . Then there was a concert with bagpipes, flutes and hautboys and, after a sumptuous banquet, country dancing which lasted until nightfall. . . . No one grumbled about unjust taxes; everybody paid his due cheerfully and I never remember hearing of soldiers plundering a
25 parish, let alone laying waste entire provinces as merciless enemies have so often done since. . . .
  Thus it was at the close of the reign of good Henri iv, whose end was the end of so many good things and the beginning of so many bad, for an angry demon took away the life of that great prince.

M. de Marolles, *Les Mémoires de Michel de Marolles, abbé de Villeloin*, Paris, 1656–7, vol i, p 11, trans. by D. Seward, *The First Bourbon*, Constable, 1971, p 160

### Questions

 a  In what ways does this passage convey a picture of Henry's reign as a golden era?
 b  Who was the 'angry demon' (line 29) who destroyed Henry?
 * c  Did the French peasantry really have 'goods and possessions sufficient enough' (lines 6–7), or is this an idealised picture of their life?
 * d  Is it true that no one 'grumbled about unjust taxes' (line 23)?
 * e  Why was Henry's reign viewed by contemporaries as 'the end of so many good things and the beginning of so many bad' (line 28)? Would historians share this view?

## 3   Richelieu on Louis XIII and Kingship

The King is good, virtuous, discreet, courageous and intent on acquiring fame, but it is [equally] true to say that he is precipitate, suspicious, envious and susceptible to sudden antipathies and first impressions to the detriment of all and sundry. . . . His Majesty must either decide to pursue
5   the affairs of state with persistency and force or must delegate his authority to some other person, in order that he may act for him. . . . And in this respect it would seem that His Majesty is jealous of his own shadow, for, just as the stars have no other light save that which they receive from the sun, so too it is His Majesty who gives his creatures
10   force; they shine only in his reflected light . . . [and] are as interested in safeguarding his person as he himself . . . , for if God were to remove him from this world, they would be exposed to all the hatred they have acquired by serving him so well. . . .

The King pays so little attention to his affairs and disapproves so readily
15   of the expedients proposed to him in order to ensure the success of those he does undertake that in future it may well prove difficult to serve him. The respect that is shown to him and the fear of offending his sensibilities stifle the very best intentions in the hearts and minds of his most capable servants. . . .
20   It is so very dangerous for the State when the application of the law is treated with indifference that I feel bound to observe that His Majesty appears to show a lack of firmness and zeal regarding the observance of his own laws, especially the edict forbidding duelling. . . . His Majesty and His Majesty's council will have to answer for all those souls who perish in
25   this diabolical way. . . . Those who fail to invoke their authority to keep their State in due and proper order are guilty before God. . . . If a King suffers the strong to oppress the weak with impunity in his kingdom . . . , if he allows men to disturb the peace of his realm . . . , he will surely perish. . . . A Christian can never forget a wrong or forgive
30   an offence quickly enough, but a King, a governor or a magistrate can never punish them quickly enough when they concern the State. . . . Man's ultimate salvation is achieved in the other world . . . [but] States do not survive this present world, their salvation is here and now or not at all, and so punishments necessary for their
35   survival cannot be deferred but must be immediate. . . .

It is a precept of great Princes to reward those who serve their States worthily; it is an investment that will be repaid ten times over. . . . [As for myself] my already depleted forces are daily reduced to such an extent that I am no longer able to endure the unbelievable strain imposed by the
40   actions that have to be taken to ensure the safety of a great State, especially when this physical strain is accompanied by great deliberations, great anxieties and great spiritual afflictions.

Richelieu's speech to Louis XIII, 13 January 1629, trans. by B. Hoy in C. J. Burckhardt, *Richelieu and His Age, vol II, Assertion of Power and Cold War*, Allen & Unwin, 1970, pp 16–23

## Questions

a  'I am master and want to be obeyed.' How do these words of Louis XIII compare with the criticisms made by Richelieu in this passage?

b  To what does Richelieu refer when he says Louis was 'jealous of his own shadow' (lines 7–8)? What reasons does he give to justify entrusting power to ministers?

c  Why was the 'edict forbidding duelling' (line 23) regarded as such an important issue?

d  He 'loved glory more than morality allows'. What does this extract tell you of Richelieu's political beliefs?

e  What 'great deliberations, great anxieties and great spiritual afflictions' (lines 41–2) faced Richelieu in his time in office?

f  Does this passage shed any light on the Day of Dupes incident?


## 4  Louis XIII Defends Richelieu

*Gaston to his brother, Louis XIII:*
Not a third of your subjects in the countryside eat ordinary bread; another third lives only on bread of oats, while the other third has not only been reduced to mendicity but languishes in such lamentable need that some die of hunger while others subsist only on acorns, grass, and similar things like beasts. Of these, the least to be pitied are those who eat only the offal that they gather from slaughterhouses. . . . It is a prodigious and shameful calamity for this state and an evil augury. God grant that the sobs that it tears from the hearts of these wretches, whose plaintive voices rise to Heaven, will not provoke its ire and will cause it to fall only on the head of the Cardinal, the sole cause of their misery.

*Louis XIII to his brother, Gaston:*
I know the qualities and capacity of those whose services I employ, and God has given me the grace to understand my affairs better than those who mistakenly attempt to interfere by discussing them. It is neither for you nor them to censure my actions and those of the men I employ in my service. . . . It is insufferable that cowardly and infamous persons should . . . be so presumptuous as to write that I am a prisoner without knowing it. . . . I have been served with such fidelity and courage by my cousin, Cardinal Richelieu, and his counsel has been so useful and advantageous to me that I can only demonstrate to everyone my complete satisfaction with the signal services that he has rendered. . . . I cannot entrust the things that concern me to better hands than his. . . . In all that has happened he has done nothing except at my express command and with complete fidelity. All his acts oblige me to tell you that he merits as much praise as your followers attempt to cast blame upon him. . . . Your followers maliciously exaggerate the misery and need of my people who are the object of my concern in all things. They seem not

to understand that the necessary and unavoidable expenditures which I
have had to make in order to avoid abandoning not only my allies but my
entire realm have been immeasurably increased by the pernicious advice
30   that they have given you.

   Letters dated April, 1631 in *Mercure francais*, vol XVII, 254—5,
   261—4, trans. in W. F. Church, *Richelieu and Reason of State*,
   Princeton University Press, 1972, pp 208—10

## Questions

*   a   Does Gaston's picture of the life of the peasants 'exaggerate the misery
        and need' (line 25) or was it a true one because of Richelieu's belief
        that 'when the people are too comfortable it is impossible to keep
        them within the bounds of their duty'?
    b   What does this extract reveal about Louis' attitude to (i) his kingship
        (ii) his relationship with Richelieu?
    c   What 'unavoidable expenditures' (line 27) had Louis XIII faced in
        support of France and her allies?
    d   Was Louis XIII correct in believing the role of Gaston and his
        supporters to be 'pernicious' (line 29)?
*   e   'He debased the King and brought honour to the reign.'
        (Montesquieu) Is this a fair estimate of Richelieu's career? (See also
        extract 3.)

## 5   The Character of Mazarin

(a)  His extraction was mean and his childhood infamous. . . . He pleased
Richelieu, who made him a cardinal . . . and he continued to act as a
kind of valet under Richelieu, notwithstanding the purple he
wore. . . . Fortune having blinded him as well as everyone else, he set
5   himself up, and was set up by others, for a Richelieu, but in his case
imitation was a piece of impudence. What the first had considered
honourable, the other thought disgraceful. He turned religion into a jest.
Nobody could be more prodigal of his promises because he intended to
break them all. He was neither gentle nor cruel, because he kept no
10   remembrance either of benefits or of injuries. He loved himself too well,
which is natural to cowardly souls. He respected himself too little, which
is the character of those who have no value for their reputation. . . . He
was a man of wit, insinuation, pleasantry and manners; but the base heart
appeared through all, so that while in adversity he seemed merely
15   ridiculous, in prosperity he had the air of a cheat. He was a pickpocket of a
statesman.

   Cardinal de Retz, *Memoirs*, Paris, 1655—65

(b)  He was of no ordinary presence: his stature rather of a neat cut than

tall, with a high forehead: one would readily judge him a mild
man. . . . So great a power had he over his countenance and language,
20  that when he would most conceal his intentions, he seemed most open-
hearted; so artificially couching his words, that a man would easily
imagine he meant to perform more than he promised. . . . His natural
abilities he improved by industry, for greater Affairs he would manage
himself, sparing of sleep and ease. . . . Being aware of the uses of money,
25  he was counted thrifty of the Publick, covetous of his own. . . . He pryed
into the Secrets of Kingdoms and private Persons. I know not whether
ever man was more accomplished to delude the French. . . . He was
wholly inaccessible even to those that were reputed his greatest
Confidents. . . . Towards prosperity and adversity he bore an even face,
30  not mind. . . . Large in promises, which oftentimes he did not
perform . . . sometimes he rewarded Vertue, but never went forth to
meet it. . . . The reputation of clemency he stood upon, even when
severity had been expedient to absolute Government. . . .
    He deserved well of our Ancestors and Posterity, having increased the
35  Empire by the accession of Territory, and not impaired it by any eminent
loss. It must be marked that he fell into times different to Richelieu's. He
had most sore Enemies that rivalled a Woman and a Child. . . . He
stoutly waged and gloriously finished a War that had been rashly
undertaken.

B. Priolo, *The History of France under the Ministry of Cardinale
Mazarine*, trans. by C. Wase, London, 1671, pp 421–4

## Questions

*a*  What criticisms does de Retz make of Mazarin? How does he
compare him to Richelieu, and why might his views be prejudiced?

*b*  Why does Priolo feel it is unfair to compare Mazarin with Richelieu?
What does he reveal about Mazarin's character, and does his view
agree with that of de Retz?

\*  *c*  'His extraction was mean and his childhood infamous' (line 1). Why
did Mazarin's background make him unpopular?

✝  *d*  'He stoutly waged and gloriously finished a War that had been rashly
undertaken' (lines 37–9). Is this an accurate description of Mazarin's
role in France's war with Spain?

\*  *e*  Do you agree that Mazarin was a 'pickpocket of a statesman' (lines
15–16)?

## 6    The Fronde of the Parlement

(a) Sire, you are our sovereign Lord; the power of Your Majesty comes
from above, and you owe an account of your actions, after God, only to
your conscience; but it is to your glory that we should be free men and
not slaves. The grandeur of the state and the dignity of the crown are

5   measured by the quality of those who obey you. . . . Formerly, the
wishes of the king were never executed without being first approved by
all the great men of the kingdom, by the princes and officers of the crown.
Now this political authority is vested in the Parlement; our possession of
this power is guaranteed by a long tradition and recognised by the people.
10  The opposition of our votes, the respectful resistance that we exercise in
public affairs must not be seen as disobedience, but rather a necessary
result of the exercise of our office and the fulfilling of our obligations. The
king's Majesty is not reduced by his having to respect the decrees of his
kingdom, because, by in so doing, he governs, in the words of Scripture, a
15  lawful kingdom.

> Omer Talon, *Mémoires*, in *Nouvelle Collection des Mémoires,*
> vol xxx, ed. by J. F. Michaud and J. J. F. Poujoulat, Paris, 1854,
> p 268

(b) Authority must be re-established at any cost, and placed higher than
before, or it will perish and be ridiculed. . . . Parlement has assumed the
functions of the King, and the people defer to it entirely. It has made
Broussel an associate of the King; it has taken up arms . . . barricaded the
20  front of the Palais-Royal, and spoken impudently to the Queen and me;
and it has made unprecedented demands, insolent proposals, to seize the
King, force my dismissal, and put the Queen in a convent. . . . Its officers
have also stirred up the other Parlements of France to revolt, urged the
people not to pay their taxes, and persuaded officials to request the
25  purchase price of their offices. . . . Commerce has ceased . . . and it is
impossible to find any money for the expenses of the war. . . . We have
reason indeed to punish them, and we must do so. . . . The King would
otherwise have cause to bring me to account for permitting his authority
to be destroyed.

> Mazarin, *Carnets*, in A. Chérvel, *Rev. Hist.*, vol iv, Paris, 1880,
> p 103

30  (c) All authority . . . belongs to us. We hold it of God alone, and no
person, of whatever quality he may be, can pretend to any part of
it. . . . The officers of the Parlement have no other power than that
which we have designed to entrust to them, to render justice to our
subjects. They have no more right to regulate . . . and take cognizance of
35  what is not of their jurisdictions, than the officers of our armies and our
finances would have to render justice, or establish presidents and
counsellors to exercise it. . . . Will posterity ever believe that officers
have presumed to preside over the general government of the Kingdom,
form councils and collect taxes, to assume, finally, the plenitude of a
40  power which belongs only to us?

> Royal Declaration, 31 July 1652, trans. by P. R. Doolin, *The
> Fronde*, Harvard University Press, 1935, pp 79–80

*Questions*

a   What was the role of Parlement? What arguments are put forward by Omer Talon, in extract (a), in favour of its claim to a say in political matters?

* b   Why were 'the people' prepared to listen to Parlement and 'defer to it entirely' (line 18)?

c   What does Mazarin say the claims of Parlement have produced in practice? Why is Broussel (line 19) signalled out for a special mention?

* d   In what ways did Mazarin seek to 'punish' (line 27) Parlement in the period 1648–52?

* e   To what war (line 26) is Mazarin referring? Why was money so desperately needed to continue it?

f   How does the Royal Declaration (extract (c)) answer the arguments put forward by Omer Talon?

## 7   The Fronde of the Nobility

They [the Parisians] had been so forewarned of the treachery of the court and of Cardinal de Retz, and they had been so persuaded to believe that Monsieur le Prince's individual peace had been made without considering their interests, that they had looked upon the beginning of this battle as a
5   comedy which was being played in cooperation with Cardinal Mazarin. The Duke of Orléans even corroborated this conviction by issuing no order in the city to go to help Monsieur le Prince . . . [but] Mademoiselle, exerting pressure on the mind of Monsieur, her father, shook him from the lethargy in which Cardinal de Retz was keeping
10   him. She went to bear his orders to the city hall that the bourgeois should be armed. At the same time she ordered the governor of the Bastille to fire his cannons at the king's troops; and returning to the Porte Saint-Antoine, she convinced all the bourgeois not only to receive Monsieur le Prince and his army, but even to go out and skirmish while his troops
15   were retreating. What finally also moved the people in favour of Monsieur le Prince was seeing so many persons of quality being brought in dead or wounded. The Duke of La Rochefoucauld wanted to take advantage of this circumstance for his side; and although his wound made his two eyes almost hang out of his head, he went on
20   horseback . . . exhorting the people to aid Monsieur le Prince and in the future to understand better the intentions of those who accused him of double-dealing with the court. That created, for a time, the desired effect; and never was Paris more partisan of Monsieur le Prince that it was then. . . .
25   Nevertheless, negotiations continued. Each faction wanted to make peace or to prevent the others from doing it; Monsieur de Chavigny . . . was of the opinion, like everyone else, that advantage should be taken of the good feelings of the people, and that a meeting

should be proposed to resolve that Monsieur be recognised as lieutenant
30    general of the State and Crown of France; that everyone inseparably unite
to bring about the Cardinal's exile; that the Duke of Beaufort be given the
government of Paris . . . and that Broussel be established in the office of
*prévôt des marchands*. . . . But this assembly, in which they believed lay
the security of their party, was one of the chief causes of its ruin, through
35    violence aimed at killing all those assembled at the city hall. . . . I cannot
say who was the author of such a pernicious plan, for all alike have
disavowed it; but in short, while the assembly was being held, they stirred
up armed men who came shouting at the doors of the city hall . . . set fire
to the doors and shot at the windows. . . . Many persons were killed, of
40    all classes and of all political groups. . . . None of this action was blamed
upon the Duke of Orléans: all the hatred fell upon Monsieur le Prince. As
for me, I think that both had used Monsieur de Beaufort to frighten those
in the assembly who were not on their side, but that indeed neither of
them had planned to hurt anyone. They promptly calmed the disorder,
45    but they did not erase the impression they had created in everyone's
mind. It was then proposed that a council be created composed of
Monsieur, Monsieur le Prince, the Chancellor of France, princes, dukes
and peers, marshals of France, and general officers of the party who were
in Paris. . . .
50        This council increased the discord instead of diminishing it because of
claims over the precedence they were to have in it; and . . . the Dukes of
Nemours and Beaufort, embittered by their past differences and by their
interest in several ladies, quarrelled over precedence in the council and
finally fought with pistols; and the Duke of Nemours was
55    killed. . . . This death . . . and the wounding of the other left the
Spaniards and Madame de Longueville's friends all the liberty they
desired to involve Monsieur le Prince. They no longer dreaded that their
proposals to take him to Flanders would be challenged. They promised
him everything he desired. . . . Paris was then more divided than ever:
60    every day the court won over someone in the Parlement and among the
people.

> *Mémoires de La Rochefoucauld*, ed. by A. Petitot and Monmerqué,
> Paris, 1826, LII, pp 160–73, trans. in O. and P. Ranum, *The*
> *Century of Louis XIV*, Harper and Row, 1972, pp 57–60

## Questions

* *a*  Why should the Parisians suspect Condé of 'double-dealing' (line 22)
with the court?
  *b*  What motives does the writer give for Paris deciding to lend aid to
Condé? What form did this aid take?
* *c*  What role was played in the Fronde by the Duke of Orléans? Why
could he and the various other factions inside Paris not agree on a
common policy to 'bring about the Cardinal's exile' (line 31)?

*d*   Why did the meeting of the factions increase 'the discord instead of diminishing it' (line 50)?

\*   *e*   Why did the court increasingly win over the Parlement and the people (line 60)?

\*   *f*   'The Fronde taught lessons in statecraft so vividly that they could not be forgotten.' (Wolf) What 'lessons' did the Fronde teach?


## 8   Reasons for War

How important it is to great states to have their frontiers well fortified. It is something especially necessary for this realm where the light-headedness of our people renders them incapable of making great conquests. On the other hand, their valour makes them invincible in
5   defense if provided with the proper positions and facilities. These can give rein to their courage without exposing them to excessive hardships, the only enemies they find too difficult to conquer. . . . There are no people in the world so little suited to war as ours . . . since patience in work and suffering, indispensable traits in warfare, are found only rarely in
10   them. . . . From this comes the fact that they are not suited to conquests which require time, nor to the preservation of [quick victories]. . . . There is never a war against France but what Frenchmen are to be found on the enemy's side, and even when fighting for their own country they are so indifferent to the public interest that they make no
15   effort to overcome their private whims. . . . They are even bored by continued success. At the beginning of a campaign. . . . they are more than men. But . . . [they] end up by getting more uninterested and softer than women. . . . They know neither how to draw advantage from a victory nor how to limit the success of a victorious enemy.

*The Political Testament of Cardinal Richelieu*, trans. H. B. Hill, University of Wisconsin Press, 1968, pp 120–2


## Questions

*a*   State in your own words why Richelieu believed the French to be unsuited for war.

*b*   Does this extract give any clue to the motivation behind Richelieu's foreign policy?

\*   *c*   What factors led Frenchmen to fight 'on the enemy's side' (line 13)?

\*   *d*   Did Mazarin share the views and aims of Richelieu's foreign policy? Was the Fronde a result of Frenchmen becoming 'uninterested' (line 17) in the continuation of war?

# II    The Thirty Years War

## Introduction

The 'traditional' view of the Thirty Years War was that it was a religious war in Germany, created by militant catholicism and the breakdown of the Religious Peace of Augsburg. This war was then exploited by the foreign powers for their own political reasons, so that Germany became 'the battlefield of Europe'. This view has long been challenged. Some have argued over the interplay between religion and politics (extracts 1 and 2), and others have refused to see it as a German war at all, because the war was never confined to a single locality and most European countries of any significance were involved. Steinberg, for example, sees the war as 'a by-product of France's efforts . . . to break her encirclement by the Habsburg powers of Spain and Austria', and he describes the whole concept of a 'Thirty Years War' as 'a figment of retrospective imagination', because there was not one war but many, lasting till 1659. Others, like Polisensky, see the war as 'two civilisations in ideological conflict', part of a 'general crisis' affecting all Europe (see section x).

Contemporaries painted a horrific portrait of destruction (extract 3). Nevertheless, the social and economic effects of the fighting are greatly disputed. The 'traditional' view was that the brutal fighting (and the resulting famine, migration, plague, etc.) destroyed towns, disintegrated the established pattern of agriculture and commerce, decimated the population so that the country did not properly recover till the nineteenth century, and brutalised the German people so that they could never become a civilised people. The 'modern' view has been to argue that the contemporary picture of destruction was exaggerated for propaganda and other reasons and that, although some areas suffered greatly, others enjoyed comparative prosperity. Germany, it is alleged, was already in decline and the war merely confirmed (or perhaps accelerated) this. Thus the declining prosperity of German towns and the deteriorating position of the peasantry stemmed from factors such as the rise of the Netherlands and the currency inflation of 1619–23. Other historians have shown that the period after 1648 was no cultural desert but a time of rich artistic and literary merit. However, concepts of economic decline or advance are difficult to define, especially in an area like Germany which does not form an economic unit, and there are no reliable statistics for the period. Some recent studies, therefore, have reaffirmed the destruction created by the war. Thus Rabb says: 'At best, the Thirty Years War started a general decline that had not previously existed; at worst it replaced prosperity with disaster', while Polisensky argues the war was 'incalculably deleterious, setting back the development of communities by nearly a century' (extract 4).

Peace was welcomed by virtually everyone. However, the national and international effects of the Treaty of Westphalia, which some see as 'Europe's first great peace congress' (Ogg), are disputed. Some historians have seen the treaty as 'the midwife of German weakness in subsequent centuries' because it created a disunited Germany (and therefore it also paved the way for French aggrandisement). Others argue the Empire was already dying and the treaty meant Austria could have become 'a powerful centralised monarchy' (Hughes) (see section v). Did the treaty in fact merely establish a European balance of power (extract 5)? On an international level, some argue the war marked the emergence of the modern state, replacing religious standards by those of secular self-interest so that later wars were waged for national security, commercial gain, or dynastic ambition. But was the triumph of *raison d' état* a consequence of the war? Or was it a product of seventeenth-century philosophy and the 'age of reason'?

The debates over the Thirty Years War continue to develop. Thus, in two recent works, Benecke concludes by saying the war produced 'no immediate, drastic social changes and no major revolutionary, democratic, or technological advances', while Polisensky concludes it 'changed the structure of European society', introducing the modern era (extract 6).

## Further Reading

The best introduction to the subject is S. H. Steinberg, *The 'Thirty Years War' and the Conflict for European Hegemony*, Edward Arnold, 1966. The other standard works are C. V. Wedgwood, *The Thirty Years War*, Cape, 1938 and Penguin, 1957; G. Pagès, *The Thirty Years War*, A.&C. Black, 1970; and J. V. Polisensky, *The Thirty Years War*, Batsford, 1971. There is a useful selection from the writings of some twenty historians in T. K. Rabb, *The Thirty Years War: Problems of Motive, Extent, and Effect*, D. C. Heath, 1964, and a useful debate between two historians in H. Kamen and M. Hughes, 'The Thirty Years War', in *European History 1500–1700*, Sussex Books, 1976. Those interested in contemporary reactions to the war should see G. Benecke, *Germany in the Thirty Years War*, Edward Arnold, 1978, and the semi-autobiographical novel by H. J. C. von Grimmelshausen, *Simplicius Simplicissimus*, John Calder, 1964. Also highly recommended is D. Maland, *Europe at War 1600–1650*, Macmillan, 1980.

## (a)  Religious Intolerance

Most gracious Prince, the unspeakeable spoyling, destruction, miserie, trouble, calamitie, and subiection of these countries, wrought and effected by the accursed Cosackes and others your Maiesties Souldiers brought into the same, together with the robbings, murtherings,
5  sackings, burnings, massacrings, and other barbarian cruelties used and committed therein, mooveth and provoketh us in the name and behalfe of our principall Lords and the whole Countrey, to take and have recourse, next unto God, to your Emperiall Maiestie, with sighes and teares. . . .
10  Boys and Women being fearefully violated and ravished, are carried prisoners away, both young and old men and women, most cruelly and terribly martired, torterd, prest, their flesh pinsht, and pulled from their bodies with burning tonges, hangd up by the necks, hands, feete, and their privy-members, women, gentlewomen, and young wenches under
15  yeeres ravished till they die, women great with child, layd so long upon the fire, untill which time as that men may see the fruit in their bodies . . . and many thousands of innocent people fearefully murthered . . . notwithstanding their Letters Pattents of assurance and protection, (because they professe the Lutheran Religion). . . .
20  Therefore, sith we know, that your Maiesty takes no pleasure in these feareful and horrible excesses . . . Wee most humbly, once againe beseech your Maiesty, in the name of our principall States, for the mercy of God, in the bleeding wounds of our Lord and Saviour *Iesus Christ*, that you would be pleased . . . to have compassion upon the necessitie,
25  miserie, and pitifull estates of your faithfull States, Subjects, and inhabitants.

> 'The Now Present Most Humble Supplication Of Certayne Of The States Of Lower Austria, Unto The Emperour', London, 1620, Bodleian Library, Oxford, printed in C.A. Macartney, *The Habsburg and Hohenzollern Dynasties*, Macmillan, 1970, pp 19—22

## (b)  Constitutional Issues

The determining context of the half-dozen major and half-dozen minor wars of this period was not the religious antagonism between German Protestants and Catholics but rather certain constitutional issues within
30  the Empire. . . . These problems had been raised, on the one hand, by the attempt of the emperor to transform the loose confederation of several hundreds of principalities and free cities into a homogenous unit under his effective authority and, on the other, by the efforts of most rulers, including the Emperor . . . to crush their medieval Estates and establish
35  monarchical absolutism. These political struggles were accompanied, overlaid and crossed by ideological conflicts between the adherents of the Roman Catholic, Lutheran and Calvinistic churches. As religion was still the pivot of men's political and social activities . . . arguments of

statecraft and political propaganda readily appeared in the guise of
religious or theological controversy. There is no doubt, however, that all
decisions of consequence were taken in the cool light of what at the time
became known as *raison d'état*.

> S. H. Steinberg, *The 'Thirty Years War' and the Conflict for
> European Hegemony 1600–1660*, Edward Arnold, 1966, p 2

## Questions

* *a* Did the Emperor Ferdinand allow the 'unspeakeable spoyling,
  destruction, miserie, trouble, calamitie and subiection' (lines 1–2) of
  his Austrian lands or have the petitioners presented an exaggerated
  picture?

 *b* What were 'Letters Pattents of assurance and protection' (lines 18–
  19)?

 *c* What arguments do the writers use to persuade Ferdinand that their
  cause is a just one?

* *d* If Ferdinand took 'no pleasure in these feareful and horrible excesses'
  (lines 20–1), what was he trying to achieve within his dominions?

* *e* What 'constitutional issues within the Empire' (lines 29–30) helped
  to create serious conflict in Germany?

* *f* What ideological conflicts existed between (i) Roman Catholic (ii)
  Lutheran and (iii) Calvinistic churches?

 *g* What arguments does Steinberg use to suggest that the war was
  guided by '*raison d'état*' (line 42)? Is there any common ground
  between his view and those expressed in the next extract?

## 2   The Involvement of Other Nations

(a) The motives of statesmen are mixed. How far did religion and how
far political ambition impel Olivares in Spain, Richelieu in France, and
Gustav Adolph in Sweden to intervene in the affairs of
Germany? . . . Professor Michael Roberts has suggested that to seventeenth-century politicians such a question would have appeared im-
properly framed: 'It was not their habit to keep politics and religion in
watertight compartments either in action or in thought.' Nevertheless
such statesmen had to make it clear that they were not jeopardising the
religious security of their fellow believers when they sided with their
foreign rivals. It would ill have become a cardinal of the Roman Church
like Richelieu to imperil the freedom of worship of German Roman
Catholics. Nor could the king of Sweden in threatening the Protestant
princes of northern Germany who were loyal to the Habsburg emperor
acquiesce in the crushing of German Protestantism.

But, on the whole, the motives of these men were political. Olivares
had devoted the whole of his life to restoring the prestige of the Spanish
Empire and fighting off its foes, whether they were Dutch Protestants or
French Catholics. In the 1630s he still had hopes of overthrowing the

Dutch and involving the emperor in his wars against them. The triumph
of the emperor in northern Germany appeared to open a way to
hemming in the Dutch by sea as well as by land. At the same time
Olivares was anxious to prevent the French from securing a foothold in
northern Italy and thus interfering with Spanish supremacy there. . . .

Richelieu had by the end of 1630 defeated all his domestic
enemies . . . and could concentrate on what was to be his life's main
work — his contest with the Habsburgs. His policy has been summed up
under three headings: to stop the further advance of the Spanish
Habsburgs in Europe. . . ; to reinforce the defences of France, that is to
say to shake off the Habsburgs' strategic stranglehold; and 'to build
bridgeheads into neighbouring states to guarantee them against the
oppression of Spain if the occasion should arise'. Hence he at once
engaged in elaborate diplomatic manoeuvres to embarrass the Habsburgs
by concluding alliances in Germany, Italy and the United Netherlands.
Later he was also to turn to the king of Sweden.

Gustav Adolf was no man's puppet. He too could claim that the object
of his policy was to shake off the stranglehold of his neighbours and to
build bridgeheads into northern Germany with the object of establishing
a semi-permanent base. His aims were above all strategic. . . . It had long
been his intention to wage war in Germany and it may be that his true
ambition was to make himself the master of northern Germany and thus
convert his kingdom into the mightiest Baltic power.

> M. Ashley, *The Golden Century*, Weidenfeld & Nicolson, 1969,
> pp 91–2

(b) A religious interpretation is the most common explanation available
from the chronicles, news-sheets, year-books and official propaganda of
the period. War and pestilence were interpreted from the pulpit as the
wrath of God. . . . To deny the strength of this religious mentality as a
basis for the thoughts and actions of those who lived in the period is to
exaggerate the power of secular and dynastic politics, with its gamut of
ambitious diplomats, ministers, soldiers and officials. . . . Of course, the
one fed the other and they were inextricably entwined. We must
remember that religion was all-embracing, and if politicians like
Richelieu or military enterprisers like Wallenstein could handle it
cynically, then they still needed it all the more as an effective ideology in
order to induce support for their decisions among subjects and ordinary
people. Politics without religion was unthinkable. Naturally, religion
had its own development: it was an all-pervading ideology of the
times. . . . To that extent we might return to saying that the Thirty
Years War was a religious conflict if only because that is how the majority
of people living through the period regarded the matter. The secular-
diplomatic and military dimensions of war were themselves an essential
part of this religious overview.

> G. Benecke, *Germany in the Thirty Years War*, Edward Arnold,
> 1978, pp 1–2

## Questions

* *a* How accurate is Ashley's assessment of the motives of Olivares and Richelieu? Were their motives essentially 'political' (line 15)?
* *b* What 'elaborate diplomatic manoeuvres' (line 32) did Richelieu engage in to limit Habsburg power, and how did this affect the Thirty Years War?
* *c* Compare Ashley's comments on the aims of Gustavus Adolphus with those found in section VIII, extract 2. How important was his involvement in the war?
  *d* What arguments does Benecke use to suggest that the Thirty Years War was a religious conflict? Does this invalidate the approach of Ashley?
* *e* In what sense did 'politicians like Richelieu or military enterprisers like Wallenstein' use religion 'cynically' (lines 50−2)?
* *f* Is it true that 'to deny the strength of this religious mentality . . . is to exaggerate the power of secular and dynastic politics' (lines 45−7)?

## 3   Grimmelshausen on the Brutality of the War

In our century — and many believe it may be the last . . . truth demands that I leave to posterity the cruelties committed in this our German war. . . .

*On the brutality of the soldiers*
The first thing that the riders did was to stable their horses. After that each
5   one started his own business which indicated nothing but ruin and destruction. While some started to slaughter, cook and fry . . . others stormed through the house from top to bottom as if the golden fleece of Colchis were hidden there. Others again took linen, clothing and other goods . . . ; what they did not want was broken up and
10   destroyed. . . . Others smashed the ovens and windows as if to announce an eternal summer. They beat copper and pewter vessels into lumps and packed the mangled pieces away. Bedsteads, tables, chairs and benches were burned. . . . Earthenware pots and pans were all broken. . . . Our maid had been treated in the stable in such a way that she could not leave it
15   any more — a shameful thing to tell! They bound the farm-hand and laid him on the earth, put a clamp of wood in his mouth and emptied a milking churn full of horrid dung water into his belly. This they called the Swedish drink. . . . The soldiers now started to take the flints out of their pistols and in their stead screwed the thumbs of the peasants, and
20   they tortured the poor wretches as if they were burning witches. They put one of the captive peasants into the baking-oven and put fire on him. . . . Then they tied a rope round the head of another one, and twisted it with the help of a stick so tightly that blood gushed out through his mouth, nose and ears. In short everybody had his own invention to
25   torture the peasants. . . . What happened to the captive women, maids

and daughters I do not know as the soldiers would not let me watch how they dealt with them. I only very well remember that I heard them miserably crying in corners here and there.

### On the brutality of the peasants
30 Before we left the woods we saw about ten peasants partly armed with blunderbusses and others occupied in burying something. The musketeers went up to them shouting, 'Halt! Halt!' The peasants answered with their guns but when they saw they were overpowered by the soldiers, they dispersed so that the tired musketeers could not follow them. The latter however dug up what the peasants had buried . . . they
35 reached a barrel, broke it open and found a man in there who had neither ears or nose but still lived. As soon as he had recovered a little . . . he told how on the previous day some of their regiment had gone out to forage and the peasants had taken six of them prisoner. Of these they had shot five dead hardly an hour ago; they had to stand one behind the other, and
40 as the bullet after piercing through five bodies did not reach him, the sixth one, they had cut off his nose and ears, after forcing him to lick the behinds of the five dead. . . . [Then] they put him in the barrel and buried him alive.

### On the brutality of the warfare
In the battle itself each one tried to prevent his own death by slaughtering
45 his nearest enemy. The horrible shooting, the rattling of harness, the crashing of pikes, and the shouts of wounded and aggressors made with trumpets, drums and pipes, a gruesome music. One could see nothing but thick smoke and dust, which seemed to veil the fearful view of the wounded and dead, and in it one heard the lamentations of the dying and
50 the gay shouting of those still full of courage. . . . The earth, whose habit it is to cover the dead, was there itself strewn with bodies. . . . Heads lay there which had lost their natural masters, whereas there were bodies with heads missing. Some had their guts hanging out, horribly and pitifully, and others had their heads smashed and the brains spat-
55 tered. . . . There lay arms shot off, on which the fingers still moved as if willing to return to battle. . . . Mutilated soldiers begged for their *coup de grâce* although certain death was close enough and others prayed for pardon and the sparing of their lives. In short, there was nothing else but a miserable and pitiful spectacle.

H. J. C. von Grimmelshausen, *Simplicius Simplicissimus*, 1669, trans. by H. Weissenborn and L. Macdonald, John Calder, 1964, pp 13, 19—20, 39—40, 148—9

## Questions
a This contemporary novelist probably permitted himself some licence in describing events, although he had witnessed some of the scenes in

his book and heard reports of the rest. What impression does he provide of life in Germany during the war?

*b* Is there any significance in his opening remark that many people believed the century might be 'the last' (line 1)?

* *c* Why was there so much conflict between soldier and peasant?

* *d* To what extent did religious fervour contribute to the barbarity of the war?

* *e* How brutal was warfare in the seventeenth century? Were other factors such as plague and famine more destructive than the actual fighting in the case of the Thirty Years War?


## 4  Historians on the Destructiveness of the War

(a)  Nothing is gained by putting the Thirty Years War in a class by itself; its destructive aspects are common to every war . . . and an impartial assessment of the facts will lead to the conclusion that some of the features most commonly attributed to it are unconnected with the war itself,
5 while others have been generalised and exaggerated . . . for the compilers of town chronicles, parish registers, family albums and personal diaries, all belonged to the same class of educated, professional men – clerks, priests, officials, lawyers – who were hit by every vicissitude of the times, and always hit hardest. . . . All the campaigns of the period
10 1609–1648 were of short duration and the armies themselves of a very small size. It was only the districts of primary strategic importance which had to bear the brunt of successive invasions. . . . Other tracts of Germany were hardly affected at all, some only for a few weeks, and the majority of towns never saw an enemy inside their walls.

S. H. Steinberg, 'The Thirty Years War: A New Interpretation', *History*, n.s. 32, 1947, pp 92, 97

15 (b)  There is no doubt that to concerned observers, the disintegrations of the Thirty Years War, the frightful spectre of total anarchy raised by the new military tactics, the unprecedented slaughter, and the lawlessness of international relations, seemed to have brought Europe to the edge of the abyss. . . . None of the wars of the previous centuries had been so
20 persistent and so totally destructive of human life for so long a period and over so wide an area. . . . The momentum that the violence built up had been so powerful that it took two years after the signing of the peace to bring the serious skirmishing to an end, and another four years to persuade soldiers to return home from their garrisons and to end their
25 state of readiness. No wonder it seemed that the avalanche of combat might shatter European society beyond recall, or that the relief at its end should have been immense enough to change the nature of warfare: to end, for a while, the 'swath of destruction' policy enunciated by Gustavus.

that helped form modern industrial society. For there is general scholarly agreement that war became 'milder' and 'more civilised' in the late seventeenth century, and that particular credit must go to the improvement of discipline, military academies, and the creation of standing
35  armies. According to Louis André, the army fashioned by Le Tellier and Louvois could not have been more different, in its acquiescence to regulation, from the disordered bands of the Thirty Years War. Occasional atrocities, such as Louis xiv's demolition of the cities of the Palatinate, were relatively rare and always planned − not the excesses of
40  marauding soldiery. Nor could the destruction of goods and life in these instances compare in magnitude with the damage to property and the killings of half a century before. Moreover, one European leader, William iii, was relentless in his insistence on restraint. Stephen Baxter has described him as the originator of 'humanitarian warfare'. . . . The
45  Spaniards were apparently not far behind. . . . By 1700 the sacking of towns and villages, so common a hundred years before, was unknown. . . . The battles of the War of the Spanish Succession were considerably less than half as murderous as those of the Thirty Years War. Despite vastly greater forces, they usually caused a fraction of the
50  slaughter, even in a major engagement. . . .
    Could it be that the decline of religious fervour tempered aggressive instincts? Perhaps; but then one comes up against a chicken−and−egg problem, and my view is that the hatreds and conflicts grew so out of hand that they simply had to be stopped for that reason. . . . Many of the
55  domestic upheavals of the 1640's and 1650's could be linked directly to the effects of the War, and it is not surprising that contemporary apprehension should have become widespread. . . . Disillusionment with violence and confrontation was the first of the changes that eventually led Europeans to stop struggling with the consequences of the
60  events of the early sixteenth century.
    T. K. Rabb, *Struggle for Stability in Early Modern Europe*, Oxford University Press, 1975, pp 119, 121−3, 145

## Questions

a  What ideas does Steinberg put forward to suggest that contemporary pictures of destruction might be exaggerated? Do his arguments affect the validity of extract 3?

* b  Rabb argues that 'none of the wars of the previous centuries had been so persistent and so totally destructive' (lines 19−20). Does Steinberg underestimate the destructiveness of the war?

* c  What evidence is there to suggest that warfare 'became 'milder' and 'more civilised' in the late seventeenth century' (line 32)?

d  What does Rabb mean by his reference to 'a chicken−and−egg problem' in line 52?

* e  Is it true that 'many of the domestic upheavals of the 1640s and 1650s

could be linked directly to the effects of the War' (lines 54–6)? (See section x.)

f  What does Rabb mean by saying the war 'led Europeans to stop struggling with the consequences of the events of the early sixteenth century' (lines 59–60)?

## 5  Mazarin on the Treaty of Westphalia

It might perhaps have been more useful for achieving a general peace if the war could have been pursued a little longer in Germany, instead of our haste to find an accommodation as we have now done. Yet this would have implied that we were in a position to prolong negotiations when
5  instead there was the threat that Sweden might have betrayed us and acted on her own urgent desire to conclude hostilities. The fear of such an unpleasant event overrode all other considerations. I think that the fear of total collapse by the Emperor which, considering his pathetic situation was unavoidably imminent, may have been enough to invite sympathy
10  from the Spaniards, cause them somewhat to soften their harsh stand, and protect him from such a blow. Whereas now they consider him to be secured by the conclusion of peace, despite the conditions, which are quite harsh to him, and they take no more notice of him, nor do they seem to worry about his position, which may otherwise have been a more
15  serious reason for bringing them to conclude peace. . . .

Furthermore, I gather from a reliable source that the Emperor . . . has assured the king of Spain . . . that this peace is certainly damaging in its hard terms, but that given the situation under which it was concluded, it is very advantageous. A great number of fortified places and lands have
20  been returned to him, which he had already lost, giving him the opportunity to save the rest, which under other circumstances would have been subject to the greatest danger. Since he has now deflected such a powerful blow and has got his breath back somewhat, he is ready at any time to take up the war again, whenever he chooses. For this there would
25  certainly be no lack of pretext, if only he could find the necessary means for his disposal.

Cardinal Mazarin in a letter to the French envoy, Servien, October 1648, in L. Bäte, *Der Friede in Osnabrück*, Oldenburg, 1948, p 147, trans. in G. Benecke, *Germany in the Thirty Years War*, Edward Arnold, 1978, pp 18–19

### Questions

a  Why did Mazarin believe it would have been useful to have continued the war 'a little longer' (line 2) in Germany?

b  What reasons does he give here for concluding peace?

*  c  What were the terms of the Treaty of Westphalia?

* *d* In what sense was Westphalia 'very advantageous' (line 19) for the emperor? (See section v.)
* *e* 'He is ready at any time to take up the war again' (lines 23 – 4). Would it be fair to say that 'Richelieu's coldly calculated exploitation of German differences left an indelible mark of hatred' between France and Germany that 'was to continue into the twentieth century' (Ashley)?
* *f* How long did the war with Spain continue?

## 6 Historians on the Importance of the War

(a) In Germany the war was an unmitigated catastrophe. In Europe . . . it was totally ineffectual in settling the problems of Europe. . . . The Peace has been described as marking an epoch in European history. . . . It is supposed to divide the period of religious
5 wars from that of national wars, the ideological wars from the wars of mere aggression. But the demarcation is as artificial as such arbitrary divisions commonly are. . . . The war solved no problem. Its effects, both immediate and indirect, were either negative or disastrous. Morally subversive, economically destructive, socially degrading, confused in its
10 causes, devious in its course, futile in its result, it is the outstanding example in European history of meaningless conflict. The overwhelming majority in Europe, the overwhelming majority in Germany, wanted no war. . . . They wanted peace and they fought for thirty years to be sure of it. They did not learn then, and have not since, that war breeds only
15 war.

> C. V. Wedgwood, *The Thirty Years War*, Penguin, 1957, pp 459–60

(b) Only the passage of time has revealed that the Thirty Years War meant the completion of one stage in the process of world history, and that Westphalia inaugurated an era where this history becomes effectively a unitary one involving the whole continent of Europe and the
20 overseas dependencies of the maritime powers. . . . It did so primarily because the War changed the structure of European society, a society which under the pressure of events during the conflict for the first time became aware of its existence and its essential unity. The War embraced all the states of Europe for greater or lesser periods of time. . . . The
25 entire continent was divided into two warring camps, for all that both coalitions were unstable and some countries wavered between them or passed from one to the other. . . . It was the first conflict where active diplomacy played an important role, and thus it meant a new stage in the evolution of international relations. . . .
30 The War was such a protracted and intensive undertaking that it demanded entirely new methods of military organization and the maintenance of armies. In other words fighting could no longer be left to private entrepreneurs on land and sea. *Condottieri* of the Wallenstein type

could not compete with the state as military employers. . . . As the size,
35  composition and equipment of armies changed, the financial sources
which supported them became the instruments of power politics. . . . It
openly displayed the very clear links between economics and politics. . . .

The War acted as a catalyst to accelerate certain socio—economic
changes which were already in progress before it broke out . . . here
40  contributing to the economic rise of the Netherlands, there creating the
preconditions for a revolutionary shift of productive relations in England,
elsewhere perhaps encouraging boom conditions in neutral countries.
Against this it meant the destruction of the middling classes in central
Europe, the temporary elimination of the nobility from private initiative
45  in places as far apart as Bohemia and Holstein, the liquidation of Johan
Skytte's land reform in Sweden's Baltic territories and the exaggeration
of the move towards a new serfdom over a large part of Europe. In time
this last point was to prove most vital of all: the West now gained a series
of advantages which the East lacked, and a further step was taken towards
50  the artificial separation of the two. . . . Thus the Thirty Years War
underlined an already existing inequality of economic development. . . .

The War changed the order of European politics and directed it into
new channels. Of the two organizational models which the men of 1618
had seen as the focus of the two belligerent camps, the United Provinces
55  and Spain, the latter had by 1648 vanished irretrievably from the
perspectives of a succeeding generation. . . . For the second half of the
seventeenth century another opposition became the axis on which
European politics turned: that between the United Provinces and France.
How and why England later replaced Holland . . . is one of history's
60  most fascinating questions. . . . It is however a fact that Great Britain and
France were to be competing models for the rest of Europe until at least
the end of the eighteenth century.

J. V. Polisensky, *The Thirty Years War*, Batsford, 1971, pp 257–
61

## Questions

a   Why does C. V. Wedgwood believe the war to have been a
'meaningless conflict' (line 11)?
*   b   Is there any evidence to suggest that the war was 'morally subversive'
and 'socially degrading' (lines 8—9)?
c   State, in your own words, the economic consequences that Polisensky
believes the war had.
d   Why did the war display 'the very clear links between economics and
politics' (line 37)?
e   What does Polisensky mean by his reference to the United Provinces
and Spain as 'organizational models' (line 53)?
*   f   According to Polisensky's Marxist approach, the war 'changed the
structure of European society' (line 21). Is this true?
*   g   Why do you think the Thirty Years War has evoked such different
responses from historians as revealed here and in extract 4?

# III  The Decline of Spain

## Introduction

'I get the impression that so much of what is written about the decline of
Spain is written with the benefit of hindsight; that because we know the
end of the story we are all looking back trying to find what we assume to
be the inevitable reasons for Spain's downfall. Supposing, for instance,
that Spain instead of France had triumphed at the Battle of Cordeville,
might we not all be writing our essays on the decline of France instead?'
So said J. H. Elliott in a recent debate, and he sounds a useful word of
warning. Spain made massive efforts to defeat the Dutch in 1600—1609
and 1621—48, and her decline was not a dramatic one for even in the mid
seventeenth century she had the largest military commitment in the
world and was still a force to be reckoned with. It is not surprising
therefore that some historians have pointed to the increasing weakness of
the Spanish monarchy as the real factor in the country's decline. Louis xiv
commented on the Spanish kings that one would think they 'had tried by
their conduct to destroy the realm rather than to preserve it'. However,
the crown inherited many problems from Spain's 'golden century'
(extract 1) and some have argued the decline stemmed from the attitudes
of Spain's aristocracy, who, as a Venetian ambassador commented, had
'no thought for the public welfare' (extract 2). Other historians do not
confine their criticisms to the nobility. Thus Williams argues: 'The make-
up and mentality of society itself seemed to predestine the Monarchy to
shipwreck. There was an undertow of decadence in the people which was
perhaps too strong for any ruler, however gifted, or any political system,
however efficient, to navigate'.

Many contemporaries, aware of Spain's decline, blamed the country's
disunity. The oath of the Aragonese Cortes to the king indicates the
problem: 'We, who are as good as you are, take an oath to you who are no
better than we . . . on condition you preserve our *fueros* and liberties, and
if you do not, we do not'. Olivares, who was the hope of the *arbistras*
wanting reform, urged Philip iv to act (extract 3), but the attempt to
centralise (or Castilianise?) Spain merely resulted in rebellion in Catalonia
and Portugal (extract 4). In any case, Olivares, though forward-looking
in his domestic policies was a man of the past when it came to his foreign
policy, because he tried to maintain Spain's imperial role — a role some

would see as crucial to understanding Spain's decline. Was the Spanish devotion to catholic orthodoxy and the political power of the inquisition crippling enough internally, without Olivares' attempt to make the country once again 'the sword of the Counter-Reformation', as well as the head of an anti-French Habsburg alliance?

One contemporary observer remarked that 'the peasant who works in the field has to support himself, his lord, the clergy, the money-lender, and all the others who batten on him', and, to most historians, Spain's decline was essentially an economic one. However, the factors behind this decline are disputed: With one-tenth of the population claiming noble status (and tax exemption) and the church (also exempt) owning one-fifth of the land, was Spain's financial policy 'nothing more than a sophisticated form of plunder'? Did Spanish agriculture not benefit from the growth of large estates because landowners were more concerned with prestige than profits? Can Spain's decline be attributed to the declining population of Castile which traditionally bore the burden of empire? Did Spanish industry not benefit from the drift to the towns because of shortage of capital, low demand, poor communications, internal tariffs, technological backwardness, or just sheer contempt for work? How important was the decline in American bullion, with its resulting repudiation of debts, debasement of the coinage, and violent inflations and deflations (extract 5)?

Some contemporary accounts are very perceptive in their analysis (extract 6) of why Spain had become 'the victim to be dismembered rather than the feared leader' (Pennington). However, even in decline, Spain retained a sense of its heritage and the hope remained that God would vindicate his people (extract 7). A new dynasty offered new hope.

## Further Reading

A good but detailed introduction is J. H. Elliott, *Imperial Spain*, Edward Arnold, 1963 and Penguin, 1970. There are very useful chapters on Spain in E. N. Williams, *The Ancien Regime in Europe, 1648–1789*, Bodley Head, 1970; P. Erlanger, *The Age of Courts and Kings*, Weidenfeld & Nicolson, 1967; and a stimulating debate in J. H. Elliott and H. Kamen, 'The Rise and Decline of Spain', in *European History 1500–1700*, Sussex Books, 1976. Also recommended are: R. T. Davies, *Spain in Decline 1621–1700*, Macmillan, 1957; H. Kamen, *The Spanish Inquisition*, Weidenfeld & Nicolson, 1965; J. Lynch, *Spain under the Habsburgs, vol II*, Oxford University Press, 1969 (some sections in vol I are also relevant); G. Parker, *The Army of Flanders and the Spanish Road 1507–1659*, Cambridge, 1972; and J. H. Parry, *The Spanish Seaborne Empire*, Hutchinson, 1965. J. H. Elliott, *The Revolt of the Catalans*, Cambridge University Press, 1963, is very detailed but it throws considerable light on Spain's problems. The best biographies dealing with the period are M. Hume, *The Court of Philip IV*, Eveleigh Nash & Grayson, new edn 1927, and J. Nada, *Carlos the Bewitched*, Collins, 1962.

## 1 The Imperial Dream

There hath bene, in all times, from the world's foundation, one chiefe commander or monarch upon the earth. . . . Our nation was, by the Bishop of Rome, selected before other peoples, to conquer and rule the nations with a rod of iron; and our kings, to that end, adorned
5 with the title of Catholike King, as a name above all names under the sun. . . . The Emperour of Russia, Rome, Germany, extend not their limits further than their stiles, which are locall, onely my master, the most Catholike king, is for dominion of bodies, as the universal bishop for dominion of soules, over all that part of the world which we call America
10 (except where the English intruders usurp) and the greatest part of Europe, with some part of Asia and Africa, by actual possession, and over all the rest, by zeal and indubitable right, yet acknowledgeth this right to be derived from the free and fatherly donation of his holynes, who, as the sun to this moon, lends lustre by reflection to this kingdome, to this king,
15 to this king of kings, my master. . . .

What he [the Spanish king] can get from any other king or commander, by any stratageme of warre or pretence of peace, he may take, for it is theirs only by usurpation, except they hold of him from whom all civil power is derived, as ecclesiastical from his
20 holiness. . . . All our peace, our warre, our treatises, marriages, and whatsoever . . . aimes at this principal end to get the whole possession of the world, and to reduce all to unitie under one temporal head, that our king may truely be what he is stiled, the Catholike and Universal King. . . . We see religion and the state are coupled together, laugh and
25 weep, flourish and fade, and participate of eithers fortune. . . . Wherein the wisdome of this state is to be beheld with admiration; that, as in tempral warre, it imployes, or at least trusts, none but natives, in Castille, Portugall, or Aragon; so in spiritual [matters], it imployes none but the Jesuites . . . to advance the Catholique Romane religion, and the
30 Catholike Spanish dominion together.

> The Duke of Lerma quoted in '*Vox Populi,* or Newes from Spayne', 1620, in *Somers Tracts,* vol II, London, 1809, pp 510–11

## Questions

* *a* Why does Spain claim a right 'to conquer and rule the nations' (lines 3–4)? Did she really desire 'the whole possession of the world' (lines 21–2)?

  *b* Who was Lerma? Does this extract shed any light on his attitude to (i) the papacy and (ii) the Dutch rebels?

* *c* What role was played by the 'Jesuites' (line 29) in Spain?

* *d* The first duty of the Spanish sovereign is 'with holy zeal befitting so Catholic a Prince to undertake the defence and exaltation of our Holy Catholic faith' (Philip IV). How important was Spain's imperial

mission in creating the conditions that led to the nation's decline?

* e How did other nations respond to the threat of Habsburg domination in the first half of the seventeenth century?

## 2 An Arbitrista's View

I assure Your Majesty that . . . improvements are very necessary, because this monarchy has reached the unhappiest condition that is believable, and it is in the most decayed and prostrate condition that has ever been seen until today. . . . Towns that only a few years ago had one
5 thousand *vecinos* [heads of families] do not have five hundred today, and in those that had five hundred there are scarcely signs of one hundred. In all these places there are innumerable persons and families that pass one or two days without eating, and others who merely eat herbs that they have gathered in the countryside as well as other types of sustenance never
10 heard of or used before. . . . It is certain, Señora, that there have been many deaths and illnesses everywhere this year, and everyone has assured me that these have been caused by mere want . . . and many families have emigrated to Madrid, where there have now gathered more poor people than have ever been seen. . . .
15 But it is a great disgrace that the ministers . . . are ignorant of these things because it is now customary for them, having spent all of their early life pleasantly and without working in a university or college, to arrive young at the leading posts in this monarchy and government. And there they are only exposed to excessive luxuries, salaries, and gifts from
20 the kings and Your Majesty . and they never come to feel sympathy for the poor. . . . [In the towns] there are at present many incapable, insufficient, and unworthy ministers. . . . These pass by without correction, because in the inspections that follow their terms in office, they know it is a well-known and current practice to negotiate with the
25 inspectors, the tax collectors and scribes, who judge the performance of each office by the money the officeholders give them. . . .

The sins of dishonesty, Señora, are without number. . . . And the time has come that the fear of punishment is regarded so lightly that even some ministers of God, the priests, walk about the streets as pimps, flirting with
30 the strumpets. . . . The thefts, Señora, that happen every day are many, but I do not see any great care in investigating or punishing them. Oaths are much more common, despite the laws published against them. Murders are very frequent. . . . Interest rates, Señora, are very exorbitant, and there are those who earn one hundred per cent interest
35 and even more, and all this is permitted. The respect for the Church is completely lost, and . . . in many places each holiday implies gathering around the churches as if they were lewd fairgrounds where public displays of merchandise are set up and trading is carried on. . . . The most wretched official [is allowed] to don more silks than a titled nobleman of

40   Castile and to compete in his costume with the most honoured
gentlemen.

'The Political Program of an Anonymous *Arbitrista*', Archivo
Histórico Nacional, Colección Jesuitas (Loyola) II—4—416, trans.
by R. Kagan in O. and P. Ranum, *The Century of Louis XIV*,
Harper and Row, 1972, pp 200—4

## Questions

* a   What factors had led to the decline in population described in lines 4—
14?

b   What criticisms does the *arbitrista* make about the king's ministers?
What recommendations is he putting forward?

* c   They 'judge the performance of each office by the money the
officeholders give them' (lines 25—6). How corrupt was the Spanish
administration, and had this corruption spread to the rest of society as
the *arbitrista* suggests (lines 27—41)?

* d   Is there any evidence to support the view that 'respect for the Church'
had been 'completely lost' (lines 35—6) in seventeenth-century Spain?
(See also extract 7.)

* e   What was the role of the *arbitrista* in Spanish society? Why were their
views largely unheeded?

## 3   Olivares on the Role of the King

*Olivares to Philip IV, 4 September 1626*
Let people recognise in your Majesty attention, resolution, a determination to be obeyed. . . . I have tried to impress this need upon
you . . . and to show you how indispensable it is for your Majesty's
conscience, for your reputation, and for the redress of the evils of the

5   Government, that you should work, or everything will sink to the
bottom, no matter how desperate my efforts may be to keep things
going. . . . There really is no other course but that your Majesty should
put your shoulder to the wheel, or commit a moral sin. . . . It is quite
impossible, without the personal aid and support of your Majesty, for me

10  to do what is necessary for the State, and this is being proved to me now
by daily experience. It may be that the reason why your Majesty will not
consent to work and do as I beg you, arises from the entire confidence you
place in me, and that if I were not here you might apply yourself more to
work, because you might not trust others as you trust me. This thought,

15  together with the zeal and desire, as God knows, I hope to serve your
Majesty, have brought me to the point of saying resolutely, that if your
Majesty will not do as I ask you, I will go away at once without asking
your leave or even letting you know I am going, even though your
Majesty may punish my disobedience by sending me to a fortress. . . . I

20    would rather risk your anger than fail in my duty. The evil is great.
Reputation has been lost, the treasury has been totally exhausted,
ministers have grown slack and venial, taught to neglect the execution of
the laws or to administer them with laxity. . . . Take, I pray you, sire, the
work into your own hands. Let the very name 'favourite' disappear. . . .

*Philip IV to Olivares, 4 September 1626*
25    I have resolved to do as you ask me, for the sake of God, of myself, and of
you. Nothing is boldness from you to me, knowing, as I do, your zeal and
love. . . . I should like to leave it [Olivares' letter] in my archives to teach
my children, if God grant me any, and other kings, how they should
submit to what is just and expedient.

Letter trans. in M. Hume, *The Court of Philip IV,* Eveleigh Nash &
Grayson, 1907, pp 178–82

## Questions

a   What does this extract reveal of the relationship between Olivares and
Philip IV?
b   What arguments does Olivares use to persuade Philip IV to take
stronger action, and how do his views compare with those of
Richelieu expressed in section 1, extract 3?
* c   To what extent does Olivares echo the criticisms of Spanish society
made in extract 2? Would it be fair to describe Olivares as 'the heir of
the *arbitristas*'?
* d   'Let the very name "favourite" disappear' (line 24). To what
extent were royal favourites a problem in seventeenth-century Spain?
* e   'I have resolved to do as you ask me' (line 25). Did Philip IV carry out
his resolve? Why did he later believe Spain's decline to be God's
punishment for his sins?

## 4   Centralisation or Castilianisation?

[Olivares wrote] 'The most important thing in Your Majesty's Monarchy is for you to become King of Spain; by this I mean, Sir, that Your
Majesty should not be content with being king of Portugal, of Aragon, of
Valencia and count of Barcelona, but should secretly plan and work to
5    reduce these kingdoms of which Spain is composed to the style and laws
of Castile, with no difference whatsoever. And if Your Majesty achieves
this, you will be the most powerful prince in the world'.

How was the castilianisation of these kingdoms to be achieved? The
Conde Duque suggested three possible ways. The first 'and the most
10   difficult to achieve, but the best if it can be managed', was to favour the
people of other kingdoms, 'introducing them into Castile, marrying
them to Castilians', and, by admitting them into the offices and dignities
of Castile, to prepare the way for a natural union. The second was for the

King to start negotiations at a time when he had an army and a fleet
15   unoccupied, so that he could negotiate from strength.

'The third way, although not so justified, but the most effective, would
be for Your Majesty — assuming you have these forces — to go in person
as if to visit the kingdom where the business is to be done; and there to
bring about some great popular tumult. Under this pretext, the troops
20   could intervene. And in order to restore calm and prevent any further
recurrence of the troubles, the laws could be reorganised (as if the country
had been newly conquered) and brought into conformity with those of
Castile.' . . .

Olivares does not simply make a plea for bald castilianis-
25   ation. . . . Elsewhere in his memorandum, Olivares has more to say [on
the first method]. 'What reason is there that these [non-Castilian] vassals
should be excluded from honour or privilege in these kingdoms? Why
should not they equally enjoy the honours, offices and confidence given
to those born in the heart of Castile and Andalusia? . . . Is it surprising
30   that, with these Castilian vassals being admitted to all the honourable
positions round Your Majesty, and enjoying the royal presence, there
should be jealousy, and discontent and distrust? There is the greatest
justification for discontent in these other kingdoms and provinces.'

> Olivares and his 'Secret Memorandum' to Philip IV, 1624, in J. H.
> Elliott, *The Revolt of the Catalans*, Cambridge University Press,
> 1963, pp 199–202

## Questions

* *a*  How important was disunity as a factor in Spanish decline? (See also extract 6.)
* *b*  Was Olivares correct in thinking that there was 'the greatest justification for discontent in these other kingdoms and provinces' (lines 32–3)?
  *c*  State, in your own words, the three ways that Olivares suggests Philip could deal with the problem of disunity.
  *d*  Does this extract throw any light on the debate over whether Olivares' policy was one of centralisation or castilianisation?
* *e*  'There to bring about some great popular tumult' (line 19). Was the revolt of Catalonia engineered, or did it arise from other factors? Why did it not lead to the reorganisation Olivares hoped for?
* *f*  'Throughout his career, the ideal and the practical, the crusading tradition and the reforming tradition, existed uncomfortably side by side' (Elliott). Is that why Olivares proved ultimately a failure?

## 5   Economic Decline: A Classic Statement

With almost complete unanimity, previous writers since the seventeenth
century have regarded the Moorish expulsion of 1609–14 as the

overshadowing cause of Spanish economic decadence. There has been common agreement that the Moors were the most industrious, intelligent, persevering, and thrifty inhabitants of Spain, 'the flower of her artisans', the cream of her agriculturalists, and almost the only subjects who did not disdain manual labour, routine operations, and prosaic toil. We are told that the expulsion of the Moriscoes utterly ruined the rice fields of Valencia, the sugar industry of Granada, and the vineyards of Spain. . . . Facts are not in accord with the accepted thesis. . . . It is difficult to see how a race largely denied educational opportunities, social privileges, civil liberties, and equality before the law could have been the most enlightened portion of the Spanish nation. . . . The price stability of most of the commodities formerly produced by the Moriscoes in the decade following their expulsion affords strong evidence that this despicable act of religious intolerance was not a major cause of economic decadence. . . . Failure of wages and prices to reflect the expulsion strongly suggests that few Moors were expelled. . . .

All economists recognise the evil effects of misgovernment even under *laissez-faire*; but, with the state intervention and paternalism prevalent in Spain, the economic consequences of progressively inferior administrations was catastrophic. It was the crushing burden of taxation resulting from costly wars, the extravagance of the royal household, the inefficiency of tax farmers and collectors, and the avidity of court favourites rather than the expulsion of the Moriscoes . . . that was an important factor in the decline of Spain. . . . The growth of large estates, the crushing burden of taxes, and the decline in consumer demand following the decimation of the population by the great plagues of 1599—1600 and 1648—50 were the major causes of agricultural decadence. . . . The illusion of prosperity created by American gold and silver in the age of mercantilism was partially responsible for the aggressive foreign policy, contempt for manual arts, vagrancy, vagabondage, luxury, and extravagance, which led to the economic decadence of the seventeenth century. . . . The numerous and sharp fluctuations in prices upset calculations, stifled initiative, impeded the vigorous conduct of business enterprise, and wreaked havoc upon the economic life of Spain.

E. J. Hamilton, 'The Decline of Spain', *Economic History Review*, vol VIII, 1938, pp 171–3, 175, 177–8

## Questions

a  What was 'the Moorish expulsion of 1609—14' (line 2)? How important were its results?

b  State, in your own words, the economic reasons Hamilton gives for Spain's decline.

\*  c  To what extent did the Spanish economy rely on 'state intervention and paternalism' (line 20)?

\*  d  Why did 'the illusion of prosperity created by American gold and silver' (lines 30—1) have such important effects on the Spanish people?

* e Why were there such 'numerous and sharp fluctuations in prices' (lines 34—5)?

* f Did Spain display 'an incapacity for economic affairs which seemed almost inspired' (Tawney)?


# 6   Spanish Decline: A Contemporary Assessment

Spain is a potent Kingdom, which has under its jurisdiction rich and fair countries, abounding with all necessaries, not only sufficient for the use of its inhabitants, but also affording a great overplus for exportation. The Spaniards also do not want wisdom in managing their state affairs, nor
5   valour to carry on a war: nevertheless this vast Kingdom has its infirmities, which have brought it so low, that it is scarce able to stand upon its own legs: among those is to be esteemed one, the want of inhabitants in Spain, there being not a sufficient number both to keep in obedience such great provinces, and at the same time to make head
10   against a potent enemy; which want is not easily to be repaired out of those countries which are under their subjection, since . . . whenever they raise some soldiers in these provinces, they cannot trust them with the defense of their native country, but are obliged to disperse them, by sending them into other parts, under the command only of Spaniards:
15   Spain therefore is scarce able to raise within itself a sufficient number of soldiers for the guard and defence of its frontier places: wherefore, whenever Spain happens to have war with other nations, it is obliged to make use of foreign soldiers, and to raise those is not only very chargeable but also the king is not so well assured of their faith as that of his own
20   subjects. The want of inhabitants is also one reason why Spain cannot now-a-days keep a considerable fleet at sea, which nevertheless is extremely necessary to support the monarchy of that Kingdom. Another weakness is, that the Spanish provinces are mightily disjoined, they being divided by vast seas and countries: these therefore cannot be maintained
25   and governed without great difficulty; for the governors of the provinces being remote from the sight of the prince, he cannot take so exact an account of their actions; and the oppressed subjects want often opportunity to make their complaints to the king. . . . The more disjoined these provinces are, the more frontier garrisons are to be
30   maintained. . . . They are also liable to being attacked in a great many places at once, one province not being able to assist another: besides this America being the treasury of Spain, is parted from it by the vast Ocean, whereby their Silver Fleets are subject to the hazard of the seas and pirates. And if it happens that such a fleet is lost, the whole government must
35   needs suffer extremely by the want of it, the inhabitants of Spain being so exhausted, as not to be able to raise sufficient sums to supply the public necessities. The Spaniards are also mighty deficient in regulating their West India trade, which is so ill managed, that the greatest part of those

riches are conveyed to other nations, whereby they are empowered to
40  chastise Spain with its own money. After the death of Philip II it has also
proved very prejudicial to Spain, that by the carelessness of the
succeeding kings, and during the long minority of this present [Carlos II],
the nobles have so increased their power, that they are now very
backward in duly assisting the king, and by impoverishing the king and
45  commonalty have got all the riches to themselves. It is also a common
disease in all governments, where the Popish Religion has got the upper
hand, that the Popish clergy is very rich and potent, and yet pretends, by a
Divine Right, to be exempted from all public burdens.

> S. Pufendorf, *An Introduction to the History of the Principal
> Kingdoms and States of Europe*, trans. by J. Crull, London, 1697, pp
> 429–31

### Questions

*a*  What reasons does Pufendorf give for Spanish decline, and why does
he single out 'the want of inhabitants' (line 20) as a particularly bad
problem?

*b*  To what extent does Pufendorf's analysis agree with those given in
extracts 2 and 5?

*  *c*  Why was the West India trade 'so ill managed' (line 38)?

*  *d*  Is it true that the nobles 'so increased their power' that they
'impoverished the king and commonalty' (lines 43–5)? Or were
Spanish rulers 'more successful in dealing with their great nobles, and
keeping them at arm's length from the real centres of political power,
than many of their contemporaries' (Elliott)?

## 7  The Will of Carlos II

Knowing ourselves to be mortal, and unable to escape death . . . we
hereby make our testament, being of sound and free judgement. . . . First,
we pray Jesus Christ our true God and Saviour, God and Man . . . grant
us mercy and offer us clemency . . . so that we may die in His Holy Faith
5  and in obedience to the Roman Catholic Church, as we have lived. . . .

As I recognise that I am under an infinite obligation before our Lord
God and that I desire the spiritual welfare of him who shall be my
legitimate successor . . . I pray and enjoin him affectionately that as a
Catholic Prince . . . he be scrupulous in matters of faith and obedient to
10  the Apostolic See of Rome; that he live and act always in the fear of
God . . . that he honour the Inquisition, assist, and favour it, because of
the care it takes in maintaining the Faith, a thing most necessary,
especially in these times when so many heresies are rampant; that he
honour and protect the ecclesiastical order, upholding and causing it to
15  keep its exemptions and immunities; . . . that he love his vassals and
subjects, securing for them every kind of benefit and prosperity . . . and

if it should come to pass (which God forbid) that one of my successors
should espouse one of those heresies condemned and rejected by our
Holy Mother the Roman Catholic Church . . . we hold and declare him
20    incapable and unable to govern and reign in all or any of our said
kingdoms and states. . . .

I also pray and enjoin my successors that during their reign they govern
with regard to considerations of religion rather than political
interest. . . . For we ourselves have preferred, and have found more
25    fitting in the great matters with which we have had to deal, to neglect
reasons of state rather than to equivocate in the least on questions of
Religion. . . .

We declare as our successor (in the event that God should call us to Him
without leaving issue) the *Duke of Anjou*, second son of the Dauphin; and
30    in this quality, we call him to the succession to our realms and lordships,
without excepting any part of them . . . and since it is our intention, and
it is also requisite for the peace of Christendom, and all Europe, and for
the tranquillity of our kingdoms, that this Monarchy remain for ever
separate from the Crown of France, we declare . . . that in the event that
35    the Duke of Anjou should die, or inherit the Crown of France . . . the
succession should pass to the *Duke of Berry* his brother, third son of the
Dauphin, in the same manner and form; and in the event that the Duke of
Berry should die, or succeed to the Crown of France, then in that case we
declare, and call to the succession, the *Archduke*, second son to our uncle,
40    the Emperor. . . .

We pray and enjoin our successors, that during the time they govern
this kingdom, they take care to avoid every superfluous expense, grant
relief to their subjects, and reduce the taxes and impositions; for even
though these are willingly granted, our subjects are nevertheless
45    overburdened with them. . . . Taxes are paid in the blood of our
subjects, and their suffering can only be justified if the revenues are
employed in defense of the Faith. . . .

And by this testament we revoke and declare null and invalid, without
effect, all other testaments, codicil or codicils, or last wills that we may
50    have made prior to this testament. . . . In attestation of which, we the
King Don Carlos, do recognise and sign it, in the city of Madrid, this
second day of October 1700.

I the King.

G. de Lamberty, *Mémoires, négotiations, traitez, et résolutions d'état,
pour servir à l'histoire du XVIIIe siècle*, The Hague, 1724, vol 1, pp
191–212, trans. by G. Symcox, *War, Diplomacy, and Imperialism,
1618–1763*, Macmillan, 1974, pp 63–6, 70–1, 73–4

## Questions

a    What does this extract reveal about Carlos II's views on (i) the
monarchy (ii) the role of the catholic church (iii) the inquisition?

*    b    Was a major factor in Spain's decline that its rulers ruled 'with regard

to considerations of religion rather than political interest' (lines 23 – 4)?

* c Why was it necessary that 'this monarchy remain for ever separate from the Crown of France' (lines 33 – 4)?

* d What 'other testaments. . . . or last wills' (line 49) had Carlos made? Why did he feel it was so vital that his successor should inherit all the Spanish lands, rather than have them partitioned between rival claimants?

* e What was the response of other nations to this will? (See also section VII, extract 7.)

* f Why has Carlos II been described as the 'last pallid relic of a fading dynasty' (Elliott)?

# IV    The Golden Age of the Dutch Republic

## Introduction

In a world of monarchies, centralising in search of absolutism, the Dutch Republic emerged in the seventeenth century as a republican federation of seven provinces, retaining their provincial sovereignty and local self-government. Kings were seen as merely 'a gang of crowned fools, who cry for nothing but fire and blood and destruction'. Moreover, in a world where agricultural production predominated and state enterprise accounted for what little trade and industry existed, the Dutch Republic was commercial and town-based, 'private enterprise at its best'. One of her rivals remarked, 'The prodigious increase of the Netherlands in their domestic and foreign trade, riches, and multitude of shipping, is the envy of the present and may be the wonder of the future' (extract 1). Was it, as some historians have argued, 'an economic miracle' that accounts for the 'Golden Age'? Some historians would stress too the importance of Holland's 'freedom', that, in a world where aggressive war, religious persecution, and intellectual uniformity were the norm, the Republic represented peace, toleration, and intellectual diversity – a place where 'you may be what Devil you will so you be but peaceable' (extract 2).

The Republic's government was of an aristocratic type, with the provincial states representing either hereditary nobles or patrician town governments dominated by that 'most remarkable social phenomena', the regents (extract 3). These staunch republicans were highly suspicious of the House of Orange, which provided the nation's military leadership and urged the need for 'an eminent head' to give central direction and control. The clash between Oldenbarnevelt, the advocate of Holland, and Prince Maurice (extract 4) is typical of the tensions within the Republic over home and foreign policies, tensions which led one contemporary to describe the Republic as 'the Disunited Provinces'. Frederick Henry tried to shift leadership away from the regents, but they reasserted themselves against his son, William II – hence the peace of 1648 and William's attempted military coup in 1650. The stadtholderless period of 1650–72 saw the reaffirmation of provincial sovereignty, and, despite the problems with England, it was arguably the period of Holland's greatest economic, intellectual, and artistic achievement. Stable government was provided by the stipendiary councillor, John de Witt, who published a strong defence of republicanism (extract 5).

However, support for the House of Orange remained, especially among those who resented Holland's dominance (extract 6), and this support came to the fore with the disastrous war of 1672. William III became stadtholder and captain-general, but his role as king of England (after 1688) meant that Dutch internal affairs were largely managed by Holland's stipendiary councillor, Anthony Heinsius, and largely over-shadowed by the wars against Louis XIV (extract 7). The fact that the three great peace conference of Nymwegen, Ryswick, and Utrecht took place on Dutch soil testifies to the Republic's central role in European diplomacy and war, but at what expense? Did the wars destroy both the Dutch economy and the nation's distinctive culture? Did William III erode that public spirit and republican integrity on which Holland's government had been based? Signs of the Republic's decline were evident to contemporaries (extract 8), but the nature and extent of it is disputed by historians. Could it be that the Dutch in the eighteenth century were merely taken over by 'the nemesis of normality' (Wilson)?

## Further Reading

The standard introduction to the period is P. Geyl, *The Netherlands in the Seventeenth Century*, (vol I, 1961; vol II, 1964), Benn, and his *Orange and Stuart 1641–72*, Weidenfeld & Nicolson, 1969, is excellent. Also recommended are: K. H. D. Haley, *The Dutch in the Seventeenth Century*, Thames & Hudson, 1972; J. H. Huizinga, *Dutch Civilisation in the Seventeenth Century*, Fontana, 1968; J. L. Price, *Culture and Society in the Dutch Republic during the Seventeenth Century*, Batsford, 1974; and C. Wilson, *The Dutch Republic*, Weidenfeld & Nicolson, 1968. There are some very useful insights in C. R. Boxer, *The Dutch Seaborne Empire 1600 1800*, Penguin, 1973. There are a number of good biographies dealing with the period, including J. Den Tex, *Oldenbarnevelt* (2 vols), Cambridge University Press, 1973, H. H. Rowen, *John de Witt*, Princeton University Press, 1978, and S. B. Baxter, *William III*, Longman, 1966. For those wishing to examine more contemporary accounts, see: Sir W. Temple, *Some Observations upon the United Provinces of the Netherlands* , ed. G. N. Clark, Oxford University Press, 1972, and H. H. Rowen, *The Low Countries in Early Modern Times*, Macmillan, 1972.

# I   The Wealth of Holland

Now of all commerces whatsoever throughout the whole world, that of the East Indies is one of the most rich and considerable . . . . What has it been, but this very navigation and traffic that has enabled the Hollanders to bear up against the power of Spain, with forces so unequal, nay, and to 5 become terrible to them and to bring them down to an advantageous peace? Since that time it is this people, who had not only the Spaniards abroad, but the very sea and earth at home to struggle with, [who] have

in spite of all opposition made themselves so considerable, that they now
begin to dispute power and plenty with the greatest part of their
neighbours . . . their East India Company being known to be the
principal support of their state and the most sensible cause of their
greatness. . . . At this day the Hollanders are the best monied people of
Europe and . . . in their country an inheritance is worth more than in any
other part of the the world.

> F. Charpentier, *Concerning the Establishment of a French Company
> for the Commerce of the East Indies*, trans. by R. L'Estrange,
> London, 1664

*Questions*

a  What was the 'peace' mentioned in line 6, and why was it
'advantageous'?
* b  Is the French writer correct in assuming that the 'most sensible cause'
(line 11) of Dutch greatness was trade with the East Indies?
* c  Why were the Dutch the 'best monied people of Europe' (line 12) and
why was an inheritance in the Republic 'worth more than in any
other part of the world' (lines 13–14)?
d  In what way had the Dutch begun 'to dispute power and plenty with
the greatest part of their neighbours' (lines 9–10)?
* e  'The warehouse of the Western world'. Is this an apt judgement on the
importance of the Republic in the seventeenth century?

## 2   Religious Toleration

It is hardly to be imagined, how all the violence and sharpness which
accompanies the differences of Religion in other Countrys, seems to be
appeased or softened here, by the general freedom which all men enjoy,
either by allowance or connivence; Nor, how Faction and Ambition are
thereby disabled to colour their Interessed and Seditious Designs with the
pretences of Religion. . . . No man here can complain of pressure in his
Conscience; Of being restrained from his own manner of worship in his
House, or obliged to any other abroad. . . . They argue without interest
or anger; They differ without enmity or scorn; and they agree without
confederacy. Men live together, like Citizens of the World, associated by
the common ties of Humanity, and by the bonds of Peace . . . with equal
encouragement of all Art and Industry, and equal freedom of Speculation
and Enquiry. . . . The visible effects of this can be seen by the continual
and undisturbed Civil Peace of their Government for so long a course of
years; And by so mighty an encrease of their people, wherein will appear
to consist chiefly the vast growth of their Trade and Riches, and
consequently the strength and greatness of their State.

> Sir W. Temple, *Observations upon the Provinces of the United
> Provinces*, 1668, ed. by G. N. Clark, Oxford University Press,
> 1972, pp 106–7

## Questions

   *a*  What does Temple believe to be the value of religious toleration?
\*  *b*  'No man here can complain of pressure in his Conscience' (lines 6−7).
      Was the Republic really as tolerant as it appeared?
\*  *c*  Is it true that 'It was liberty of conscience for all that made for free
      enterprise' (Ashley)?
\*  *d*  'Continual and undisturbed Civil Peace' (lines 13−14). Was the
      Dutch Republic affected by the alleged 'general crisis' of the
      seventeenth century (see section x)?

## 3   The Regents

Those Families which live upon their Patrimonial Estates in all the great
Cities, are a People differently bred and manner'd from the Traders,
though like them in the modesty of Garb and Habit, and the Parsimony
of living. Their Youth are generally bred up at Schools, and at the
5  Universities of *Leyden* or *Utrecht*, in the common studies of Human
Learning, but chiefly of the Civil Law, which is that of their
Countrey. . . . The chief end of their Breeding, is, to make them fit for
the service of their Countrey in the Magistracy of their Towns, their
Provinces, and their State. And of these kind of men are the Civil Officers
10  of this Government generally composed, being descended of Families
who have many times been constantly in the Magistracy of their Native
towns for many Years, and some for several Ages.
    Such were most or all of the chief Ministers, and the persons that
composed their chief Councils, in the time of my residence among them,
15  and not men of mean or Mechanick Trades, as it is commonly received
among Forreigners, and makes the subject of Comical Jests upon their
Government. This does not exclude many Merchants, or Traders in
gross, from being often seen in the Offices of their Cities, and sometimes
deputed to their States . . . But the generality of the States and
20  Magistrates are of the other sort; Their Estates consisting in the Pensions
of their Publick Charges, in the Rents of Lands, or Interest of Money
upon the *Cantores*, or in Actions of the East-Indy Company, or in Shares
upon the Adventures of great Trading-Merchants.
    Nor do these Families, habituated as it were to the Magistracy of
25  their Towns and Provinces, usually arrive at great or excessive
Riches. . . . They content themselves with the honour of being useful to
the Publique, with the esteem of their Cities or their Countrey. . . . The
mighty growth and excess of Riches is seen among the Merchants and
Traders, whose application lyes wholly that way, and who are the better
30  content to have so little share in the Government, desiring only security in
what they possess. . . . Yet these, when they attain great wealth, chuse to
breed up their Sons in the way and Marry their Daughters into the
Families of those others most generally credited in their Towns, and
versed in their Magistracies; and thereby introduce their Families into the

35 way of Government and Honour, which consists not here in Titles, but in
Publique Employments.

> Sir W. Temple, *Observations upon the Provinces of the United
> Provinces*, ed. by G. N. Clark, Oxford University Press, 1972, pp
> 83–5

## Questions

*a* What, according to Temple, were the characteristics of the regents as
a class?

*b* Outline the evidence Temple offers of their social and cultural
background.

\* *c* Why did foreigners make the Dutch government 'the subject of
Comical Jests' (line 16)?

*d* What were the '*Cantores*' (line 22)?

\* *e* Were the merchants really 'content to have so little share in the
Government' (line 30)?

## 4 Oldenbarnevelt Defends his Policies

Most Serene and High-Born Prince, Gracious Lord, Gracious Prince and
Lord,

I observe with the most profound vexation that Your Excellency has
become totally estranged from me. . . . Nevertheless, in all sincerity and
5 honesty, I affirm that I do not know when I gave reason for such a change
of heart. I have always been and still am Your Excellency's most faithful
servant. . . . Ten years ago, when we were negotiating for a peace or
truce, I did indeed remark the beginnings of such a change. May Your
Excellency be so kind as to recall, however, that . . . [ this truce] enabled
10 the affairs of Your Excellency, your notable house, and your beloved
brothers and sisters to be put in order. During the time it has been in force,
this truce has brought the country prosperity, increased revenues, and
won for it a lofty and admirable reputation . . . as is well known and as
has been irrefutably demonstrated by the excellent alliances made after
15 the truce with various potentates and republics. These ties have in their
turn brought the friendship, counsel, and assistance of other great
potentates and republics to this country at various times. The truce also
enabled us to slow and halt the accumulation of debts, which formed a
heavy burden upon the country and the provinces. . . . In addition, this
20 country has paid off its debts to its neighbours and has repossessed the
cities and forts which had been given in pledge. . . .

Two problems have troubled the country, however. The first was the
dispute raised by the States of Zeeland several years before the truce and
continued for many years afterwards over paying its share of the national
25 budget. . . . The second problem was the disputes over doctrine and
authority in religion . . . involving Professors Gomarus and Arminius of

the University of Leiden and their respective adherents. . . .

At first we had hoped that we could settle this conflict by means of a compromise to be arranged by a legal and impartial assembly of the province of Holland and West Friesland, but it could not be done because some of the churchmen exerted such influence upon the government in a few cities that these refused to permit the States of Holland and West Friesland, who are the lawful sovereigns of this province, either to convene or direct or approve the activities of such an assembly. . . . For this reason the States were compelled to issue a provisional order that those who could not in good conscience teach, hold, or believe the doctrine of predestination or its corollaries, except as these were held by the Remonstrants, should no longer be molested, prevented from holding services, or interfered with in their performance, while those who wished to teach or hold a stricter and different position remained free to do so. . . . The States then gave repeated orders to practice mutual Christian tolerance . . . so that no split resulting from these differences of opinion would be permitted or tolerated. Your Excellency knows that I spoke of this to him many times, exhorting him that it was his duty to support my Lords the States in this matter. . . . I demonstrated that the pressure for holding a national synod was a violation of the rights of the provinces, of the Union of Utrecht, and of other treaties and of precedent, so that it would probably bring no advantage but rather great difficulties. . . .

But if Your Excellency wishes to follow the counsels of the authors of the *Necessary Discourse* and *The Spanish Counselor* [two pamphlets directed against Oldenbarnevelt] and similar seditious, slanderous, and lying pamphlets, which God forbid, then I must declare frankly and according to my own opinion, but respectfully and subject to correction, that the result cannot but be the total ruin and downfall of this country, of Your Excellency, of his esteemed House and its members, of all pious patriots, and of the true Christian religion. . . .

I am very sorry that in recompense for my long and manifold services and tasks, I am attacked by so many slanderous, lying, seditious, and fraudulent libels, and that these vicious and absurd falsehoods derive their pretext and nourishment from the ill-feeling which Your Excellency is supposed to bear toward me. . . . I find myself compelled to publish a statement in defence of myself and my family. . . . Placing my hope in this, I pray God the Almighty Lord, to preserve you, most serene and high-born Prince, in prosperity and health under his holy protection.

From my chamber, April 24, 1618.

Your Princely Grace's most humble servant,

John Van Oldenbarnevelt.

A. J. Veenendaal, ed., *Johan van Oldenbarnevelt: Bescheiden*, vol III, The Hague, Martinus Nijhoff, 1967, pp 381 — 8, trans. by H. H. Rowen, *The Low Countries in Early Modern Times*, Macmillan, 1972, pp 116—19, 122—5

*Questions*

a   What was the truce of 1609, and what arguments does Oldenbar-
     nevelt use in favour of it?
b   What were the 'excellent alliances' (line 14) made after the truce?
*  c   Why were there problems over the share paid by provinces to the
     national budget?
*  d   What were the different views of Gomarus and Arminius?
*  e   Who were the 'Remonstrants' (line 38)? What constitutional as well
     as religious arguments lay behind the controversy outlined by
     Oldenbarnevelt?
f    What fears for the future of the Republic does Oldenbarnevelt
     express? What fears for his own position does he indicate?

## 5   A Defence of the Republic

Seeing the true interest of all countries consists in the joint welfare of the
governors and governed . . . we are therefore to know that a good
government is not that where the well or ill-being of the subjects depends
on the virtues or vices of the rulers but (which is worthy of observation)
5  where the well or ill-being of the rulers necessarily follows or depends on
the well or ill-being of the subjects. For seeing we must believe that in all
societies or assemblies of men, self is always preferred; so all sovereigns or
supreme powers will in the first place seek their own advantage in all
things tho' to the prejudice of the subject. . . .
10    Such princes as are wise, and do not trust their power in other men's
hands, will not omit to strengthen their dominions against their
neighbours as much as possible. But when monarchies or republicks are
able enough to do this, and have nothing to fear from their neighbouring
states or potentates, then they do usually, according to the opportunity
15  put into their hands by the form of their government, take courses quite
contrary to the welfare of the subject. For then it follows . . . that the
next duty of monarchs, and supreme magistrates, is to take special care
that their subjects may not be like generous and meddlesome horses
which where they cannot be commanded by the rider, but are too head
20  strong, wanton, and powerful for their master, they reduce, and keep so
tame and manageable, as not to refuse the bit and bridle, I mean taxes and
obedience. For which end it is highly necessary to prevent the greatness
and power of their cities, that they may not out of their own wealth be
able to raise and maintain an army in the field, not only to repel all foreign
25  power, but also to make head[way] against their own lord. . . .
    And though weak, voluptuous, dull and sluggish monarchs neglect all
these things, yet will not the courtiers who govern in their stead, neglect
to seek themselves, and to fill their coffers whether in war or peace; and
thus the subjects' estates being exhausted by rapine, those great and
30  flourishing cities become poor and weak. And . . . those favorites omit

no opportunities to divest those populous cities of all fortifications, provision, ammunition of war, and to hinder the exercising of the commonality in the use of arms. Since it appears from the said maxims, that the publick is not regarded but for the sake of private interest; and
35 consequently that is the best government where the chief rulers and magistrates and likewise all others that serve the public either in country or city, may thereby gain the more power, honour, and benefit, and more safely possess it, whether in peace or war: and this is the reason why commonly we see that all republicks thrive and flourish more in arts,
40 manufactures, traffic, and populousness and strength, than the dominions and cities of monarchs, for where there is liberty there will be riches and people. . . .

And therefore I conclude that the inhabitants of Holland, whether rulers or subjects, can receive no greater mischief in their polity, than to
45 be governed by a monarch, or supreme lord: and that on the other side, God can give no greater temporal blessing to a country in our condition, than to introduce and preserve a free commonwealth government.

> John de Witt (really by P. de la Court), *The True Interests and Maxims of the Republick of Holland and West Friesland*, London 1702, pp 1–6, in O. and P. Ranum, *The Century of Louis XIV*, Harper & Row, 1972, pp 142–4

## Questions

a  What does de la Court argue are the disadvantages of monarchy, whether it be strong or weak?

b  Compare these arguments with those in favour of monarchy found in section VI, extract I.

c  Why does de la Court feel that monarchs have to seek war? Does section VII, extract I show some of his fears are justified?

* d  Which elements of Dutch society supported the views expressed here, and which supported those given in the next extract?

# 6  A Defence of the House of Orange

It is well known to the entire world that since the absence of an eminent head as a result of the death of Prince William II, various defects have arisen in the government which apparently can be remedied only by restoring and re-establishing an eminent head to lead it.

5  These shortcomings exist in various parts of the government, especially in the questions of military movement orders and the common army, the conduct of secret correspondence, the proposal and supply of quotas for the Union, and other points. . . .

Furthermore, whenever in these times disputes or disturbances arise
10 between some of the provinces, the state is deprived of the means of conciliation, which the earlier Princes of Orange as heads of the provinces

were able with great success and vigour to employ in overcoming these dissensions.

15 And because it is usual in all communities and societies to entrust the conduct of affairs to a few, so we can now clearly see that many parts of the functions which were exercised by the aforesaid heads have now fallen into the hands of a few who are not qualified to perform them. . . .

Your Noble Great Mightinesses during conferences on this affair have considered it not improper to say that attention should be paid to the
20 interests attaching to the present Prince of Orange. But these are such at the present time that the state need have no anxieties concerning them.

First, His Highness is connected by blood to the House of Orange and Nassau, to which these provinces . . . are in debt for their expenditure of life and property and their indomitable courage which so mightily
25 contributed to the victory of these lands and the vindication of their freedom, their rights, and privileges, and the practice of the true Reformed religion.

Second, this state has a special interest in the alliance of the House of Orange with the House of Brandenburg, because of its possessions and
30 places on the frontier of these provinces, as well as in Pomerania and Prussia on the Baltic Sea. Furthermore, the Elector of Brandenburg is not only one of the most powerful and eminent Imperial princes but is also the only one remaining who professes the Reformed religion. . . .

Among the other alliances on the side of the Princess Royal [widow
35 of Prince William II and sister of Charles II of England] is the crown of France, which has always had many interests in common with this state and which cannot be separated from it without notable difficulty and hurt for both sides.

But most important in this connection is the family tie with His
40 Majesty, the King of Great Britain, and his brothers. For anyone with ordinary and healthy understanding has sufficient knowledge of how much this country needs the friendship and good understanding of that country and nation, as sad experience has brought painfully home to the good inhabitants of this country, as they still well remember.

Lieuwe van Aitzema, *Saken van Staet en Oorlogh*, vol IV, The Hague, Johan Veely *et al.*, 1669–72, pp 638–9, 641, trans. by H. H. Rowen, *The Low Countries in Early Modern Times*, Macmillan, 1972, pp 199–200

## Questions

a   Why does the writer argue in favour of an 'eminent head' (lines 1–2) rather than a monarch?
b   What, according to this extract, are the disadvantages of not having an 'eminent head'?
c   What reasons does the writer give for regarding the Prince of Orange as a suitable leader for the Republic?
d   Who were the 'Noble Great Mightinesses' (line 18)?

* *e* What was the 'sad experience' with regard to England, referred to in line 43?
* *f* Did William III justify the fears expressed in extract 5 or the hopes expressed in this extract?

## 7   The Character of William III

(a) He has a great application to affairs, and turns them much in his thoughts; and indeed perhaps too much, for his slowness in coming to a resolution is much complained of. But if he is slow in taking up a resolution he is firm in adhering to it. . . . He is the closest man in the world, so that it is not possible so much as to guess at his intentions till he declares them. He is extreme calm both in council and actions. . . . His courage does not sink with misfortunes. . . . He understands the government of Holland exactly, and if he does stick in some things too close to his rights as he is stadtholder, yet he has often assured me that he has never gone beyond them. . . . He seems to have a real sense of religion. . . . He has a true notion of government and liberty, and does not think that subjects were made to be slaves. . . . His martial inclination will naturally carry him, when he comes to the crown of England, to bear down the greatness of France.

> G. Burnet, 1687, in H. C. Foxcroft, *A Supplement to Burnet's 'History of my own Times'*, Oxford University Press, 1902, pp 190−2

(b) King William of England was wholly occupied in calling all Europe to arms against France and Spain. . . . Grown old before his time by excessive labours in the affairs of State that were his life-long all-absorbing passion, and to which he brought such consummate skill, such masterly genius, King William had come to possess supreme authority in Holland, the English throne, the trust, nay the absolute dictatorship of all Europe, save only France. . . . When dying, religion occupied his mind as little as throughout his life. . . . Being solely concerned with the affairs of this world, he saw the end approach without misgiving. He had the satisfaction of leaving his Grand Alliance so firmly based that he had no fear of its disuniting after his death. . . . [On the news of his death] the bulk of the English nation mourned for King William, and so did most of the inhabitants of the United Provinces; but a few good republicans signed with relief at having once more regained their freedom. . . . Heinsius, his confidential agent, whom he had raised up to be Grand Pensionary, kept his memory green, and urged on the leaders of the Dutch Republic, their generals and allies, to such effect that it appeared almost as if William had not died.

> Saint-Simon, 1702, in *Historical Memoirs of the Duc de Saint-Simon*, vol I, trans. by L. Norton, Hamish Hamilton, 1967, pp 188−90

## Questions

a   What different beliefs are expressed here concerning William's religious attitude and political ideas?

* b   'He is extreme calm. . . . His courage does not sink with misfortunes' (lines 6—7). Did William save the Republic in 1672?

* c   'Wholly occupied in calling all Europe to arms' (lines 15—16). Was this an obsession that greatly damaged the Republic or a vital response to the French threat?

* d   In what sense did William achieve the 'absolute dictatorship' (line 20) of Europe?

* e   'Good republicans sighed with relief' (lines 27—8). Is it true that 'under William the erosion of the old republican virtues accelerated' (Miller)?

* f   What role did Heinsius, 'his confidential agent' (line 29), play in Dutch affairs?


## 8   The Republic in Decline

The commerce of the United Provinces in Europe has never been in a worse condition than today. During the course of earlier wars, although Dutch vessels were also open to the attacks of privateers, at least they could take refuge in the Atlantic and in the Mediterranean in ports under
5   Spanish rule, which now are closed to them. Furthermore, even when they were completely barred from the trade of France, they still continued to ply both the Baltic trades, which they continue to enjoy, and the trades of Spain, the kingdoms of Naples and Sicily, and Spanish Flanders, which now they have good reason to miss. Not only is the
10   market greatly reduced for their cloth, both of their own manufacture as well as that made in India and in the Baltic, and for their other wares, spices, salt fish, etc., but they are also deprived of the profitable return trade in wool, wine and other necessary commodities.

It is true that their trade to the Indies has not fallen off as badly, yet the
15   lack of consumers is causing difficulties like those in their European commerce. In the East Indies the Company has launched a violent war against the Mogul, and in the West Indies trade is possible only through intermediaries and hence is subject to many disturbances. In peacetime the Dutch used to earn as much as eighteen million from Cadiz when the
20   fleets (from Spanish America) returned. Smuggling does not produce anything like that amount, and the delays discourage the richer merchants, who await better times to risk their wealth. As a result, there are frequent bankruptcies, word of which scares people and discourages them from entrusting their money to merchants, whose own funds are
25   limited, as they are in the habit of doing in peacetime. This decline even affects the domestic commerce of the country, which is suffering badly, especially thanks to the cunning manipulations of the English, who take

advantage of the opportunity to raise themselves upon the ruins of their allies. . . .

30     It might be thought that the opening of trade with France would bring some solace to the United Provinces. Yet it is not to be denied that while the reduction in the price of wine has increased its sales and improved the business of a few merchants, it has ruined others whose stores were well stocked. . . .

35     Considering all the wounds which Dutch trade has received from every side, one might naturally expect that money would be in very short supply in their provinces. But we know that it circulates easily which is explained by the immense sums which were amassed by their customary trade to every part of the world. There are many individuals whose
40     wealth has not been exhausted by continued warfare, because they are sparing with what they have and renew it in business, but it would be wrong to believe that the state, who has been exhausting itself by spending so much for so long, is as rich in proportion as some of its people. On the contrary, it is extremely encumbered with
45     debt. . . .

The States of this province, in order to discharge a part of these enormous debts and to meet the exorbitant expenses of the present war, have recourse to two means which are always employed in such circumstances, that is, new taxes and more loans. There are few countries
50     where the ordinary taxes are more numerous and heavier than in Holland; taxes are collected on everything, with harshness and violence. . . . We will skip over a large number of taxes, which it would be tedious to give in detail, to discuss the so-called Hundredth Penny, which provides the state with its readiest revenues. It is collected on a
55     permanent basis from all real estate possessed by subjects of the States of Holland, which includes land, houses, contracts of indebtedness, interest-bearing bonds, shares in the East India Company, etc. . . . [and] it provides to the state every year an eighth of all revenues from the property taxed. . . . If this tax seems hard in peacetime, it is infinitely
60     worse during war. Then each possessor of real estate pays the eighth twice, that is, a quarter of his income, yet it is called the Two-Hundredth Penny. When a war takes a turn for the worse . . . the funds are found by doubling the tax of the Two-Hundredth Penny, that is, each landowner is compelled to pay out half of his annual income. This is the current
65     practice. . . .

The second resource of the province of Holland is to borrow from its own subjects. . . . Indeed, they have been fortunate enough to be able to borrow as much money as they needed until now at four percent. . . . But in the end this is not an inexhaustible stream; it must run
70     out some day if the trade which is its source itself continues to suffer from a drought. The East India Company alone, which would seem enough to prevent poverty, is scarcely able to maintain itself . . . and the Dutch are beginning to become angry against the heavy burden of the Two-Hundredth Penny, which has lasted too long.

A. E. Helvetius, *Mémoire sur l' état présent du Gouvernement des Provinces Unies*, ed. M. van der Bijl, *Bi jdragen en Mededelingen van het Historisch Genootschap*, vol 80, 1966, pp 171—80, trans. by H. H. Rowen, *The Low Countries in Early Modern Times*, Macmillan, 1972, pp 226—32

## Questions

a  What does the writer believe has happened to the Republic because of its war with France and Spain?

\* b  What problems faced the Dutch East India Company at this time?

\* c  What were the 'cunning manipulations of the English' (line 27)?

d  Why was the 'Hundredth Penny' such a burden? What other ways could the Dutch raise money?

\* e  Was the Dutch economy still a sound one by the end of the seventeenth century, or is this contemporary picture of decline an accurate one?

# V The Decline and Rise of the Austrian Habsburgs

## Introduction

To contemporaries the decline of the Austrian Habsburgs seemed as obvious as the decline of Spain. The Peace of Westphalia in 1648 marked the dynasty's political failure to subdue the German princes and its religious failure to defeat the German protestants. Instead the Holy Roman Empire was reduced to a loose federation of sovereign princes under the nominal leadership of the emperor. Moreover, the Thirty Years War had clearly revealed the inability of the emperor to defend the German states against foreign intervention, and therefore it encouraged Brandenburg, Saxony, Bavaria, and other German states to develop their own resources, so that the Habsburgs were forced to treat them more like foreign powers than part of an empire. The advance of French power is often seen as a measure of Austrian decline – thus, for example, the partition treaty of 1668 has been described as 'a confession of weakness' (Maland). Yet is this picture of Habsburg decline totally justified? Was not the concept of the Holy Roman Empire outmoded anyway? And did not its hastened demise at Westphalia have its advantages? Did not the Habsburgs emerge from the Thirty Years War with their power strengthened in their Austrian lands and established in their Bohemian lands? Did not the dynasty 'continue to pursue the same two ends – absolutism in government and regimentation in religion – but in a more restricted sphere' (Williams)? There may be a great deal of truth in the remark of Leibnitz that: 'When the Empire began to sink, God awakened a new power in Austria'.

Religion obviously played a major role in the lives of the emperors. Ferdinand II has been described as 'the heart and soul of the Counter-Reformation' (McCartney) and his Edict of Restitution in 1629 was a great statement of both Habsburg catholicism and imperial absolutism (extract 1). He and his successor, Ferdinand III, ruthlessly destroyed the protestant religion in their Austrian lands and in their Bohemian lands (extract 2). On the other hand, some historians have argued that Ferdinand II was not 'the paranoid bigot some writers have portrayed' but 'a realistic politician who was seeking to make a reality of his power in central Europe' (Hughes). Certainly the revised constitutions imposed on Bohemia and Moravia left their Estates little power, though the vital battle over taxation had yet to be fought. Indeed, it is arguable that

Ferdinand II achieved more power within the Empire than any emperor since, and including, Charles V. Some see Ferdinand III's reign as 'a sort of interregnum, a pause for breath between two great historical movements' (Crankshaw) because, if political and religious mastery was their aim, the Habsburgs had to tackle both the French and Turkish challenge, and this was to be the work of Leopold I. He took action against the Hungarians (extract 2) after their ill-fated attempt to acquire the crown of Poland, but then had to do a *volte-face* to ensure they did not join the Turks (extract 3), who were staging an impressive revival at this time. It could be argued that the Turkish declaration of war (extract 4) and the resulting siege of Vienna (extract 5) marked a major turning-point. Did, for example, the Habsburg victories that culminated in the battle of Zenta in 1697 help create 'a great new world power' (Spielman) by finally permitting the conquest of the Hungarians and a more active anti-French policy?

Leopold I attributed most of the ills of Europe to Louis XIV (extract 6, and section VII, extract 5), but war placed an immense strain on a monarchy renowned for its financial weakness and for an administration in Vienna composed of 'the biggest asses I have ever seen in my life' (Prince Eugene). The Dutch ambassador remarked in 1703 that the Habsburg monarchy was 'on its last legs and will go down in a general military collapse unless there is a miraculous intervention of the Almighty'. The miracle came in the form of the victories of Eugene and Marlborough, and not only did the government overcome an attempt for Hungarian freedom, but it emerged from the War of the Spanish Succession as a great European power. Like a phoenix, it had risen from the ashes. The political structure of the new Austrian Empire was apparently established by the Pragmatic Sanction, though the question remained: how would the Habsburgs solve the problems created by diversity of race, religion, and culture?

## Further Reading

Good introductions to the period can be found in E. Crankshaw, *The Habsburgs*, Weidenfeld & Nicolson, 1971; V. Tapié, *The Rise and Fall of the Habsburg Monarchy*, Pall Mall Press, 1971; and E. N. Williams, *The Ancien Regime in Europe*, Bodley Head, 1970. There are not, however, many books dealing specifically with the seventeenth-century Habsburgs, except for the detailed and informative R. J. W. Evans, *The Making of the Habsburg Monarchy 1550–1700*, Clarendon Press, 1979, and the biography by J. P. Spielman, *Leopold I of Austria*, Thames and Hudson, 1977. For the Turkish problem it is worth seeing P. H. Coles, *The Ottoman Impact in Europe*, Thames and Hudson, 1968; D. M. Vaughan, *Europe and the Turk 1350–1700*, Liverpool University Press, 1954; and J. Stoye, *The Siege of Vienna*, Collins, 1964. For the Habsburgs and Europe the best book is H. G. Koenigsberger, *The Habsburgs and Europe*, Cornell University Press, 1971. Also recommended is N. Henderson, *Prince Eugen of Savoy*, Weidenfeld and Nicolson, 1964. Those interested in seeing further documents should consult C. A. Macartney,

The Habsburg and Hohenzollern Dynasties in the Seventeenth and Eighteenth Centuries, Macmillan, 1970.

## 1  The Edict of Restitution

We, Ferdinand, by the grace of God, Holy Roman Emperor, etc., are determined for the realization both of the religious and profane peace to despatch our Imperial commissioners into the Empire; to reclaim all the archbishoprics, bishoprics, prelacies, monasteries, hospitals and endow-
5  ments which the Catholics had possessed at the time of the Treaty of Passau [1552] and of which they have been illegally deprived; and to put into all these Catholic foundations duly qualified persons so that each may get his proper due. We herewith declare that the Religious Peace [of 1555] refers only to the Augsburg Confession as it was submitted to our
10  ancestor Emperor Charles v on 25 June 1530; and that all other doctrines and sects, whatever names they may have, not included in the Peace are forbidden and cannot be tolerated. We therefore command to all and everybody under punishment of the religious and the land ban that they shall at once cease opposing our ordinance and carry it out in their lands
15  and territories and also assist our commissioners. . . . Should they not carry out this behest they will not only expose themselves to the Imperial ban and to the immediate loss of all their privileges and rights without any further sentence or condemnation, but to the inevitable real execution of that order and be distrained by force.

Edict of Restitution, 1629, trans. in E. Reich, *Select Documents*, London, 1905, pp 234–5

### Questions

a  What was the Holy Roman Empire and what function did the 'Emperor' (line 1) play?
* b  'To reclaim all . . . which the Catholics had possessed' (lines 3–5). What effects did this redistribution of German territory have?
* c  What had been the significance of the 'Religious Peace' (line 8)?
* d  Was this edict a turning-point in the Thirty Years War because it contained 'the threat of despotism which alienated many German dynastic territories' (Benecke)?

## 2  Persecution

### (a) *In Bohemia*

You have utterly destroyed our home, our ancient kingdom, and have built us no new one in its place. Woe to you! Some day you will have to render an account for the heritage you have received. How rich it was when you had it all men know, and you have brought it but ruin and

5  disgrace. The nobles you have oppressed, great cities made small. Of smiling towns you have made struggling villages, of pleasant towns rows of wretched hovels. Where before happy craftsmen laboured, now hungry starving wrecks of men stalk the weeded paths. . . . I can call all the extortion and violence which I see going on every day nothing else
10  than pillage. The court at Vienna, its appetite whetted by the sweet savour of Czech money, cries out daily: 'Give us more, Give us more'. . . . [And] if they see a castle being repaired, or any sort of a group of retainers, if they see any prosperity among the nobles, they immediately conclude that it is all part of preparations for a new revolt.
15  They think that the forests, the woods and the valleys, yes, even the leaves and branches of the trees cry out: 'Rebellion, rebellion'.

> B. Balbin, *Dissertio Apologetica prolingua Slavonica praecipue Bohemica*, 1670, trans. in S. Harrison Thomson, *Czechoslovakia in European History*, Princeton University Press, 1953, pp 115–16

### (b) *In Hungary*

They first stript and robbed them [the Protestant ministers] of any money they had, then they did put them in stinking prisons, they were also forced to serve perpetually, both in the hardest and the filthiest tasks that
20  could be invented, such as the cleaning of privies and all other work along the Town-walls, or Ditches. They fed them with black course Bread and Water, this last being often denied them in any abundance, none were suffered to give them Alms, or so much as to speak to them: and which was more bitter than all the rest, they were daily forced, (sometimes
25  dragged by the hair of the Head, and sometimes driven violently with Pikes and Musquets) to be present at the *Popish* Worship . . . and yet God so strengthened them, that they would never joyn in their Worship. In a word the cruel usage they met with was such, that none but Inhumane, or Savages, could so torment the brute Beasts, as their Persecutors did those
30  faithful Servants of Christ.

But when their enemies saw that they could not gain their end from those Witnesses . . . they resolved on the last Trial, which had long been threatened, and that was to send them to be Gallie-slaves. . . .

> 'A short Memorial of the most grievous sufferings of the Ministers of the Protestant Churches in Hungary by the insti-gation of the Popish clergy there', London, 1676, quoted in C. A. Macartney, *The Habsburg and Hohenzollern Dynasties in the Seventeenth and Eighteenth Centuries*, Macmillan, 1970, pp 51–2

### Questions

a  What do these extracts reveal of the nature of Habsburg rule?
*  b  'They laugh at our finances, while, for my part, I weep over them' (Prince Eugene). How poor was the financial system of the Habsburgs and does this explain why they had to 'pillage' (line 10) Bohemia for money?

* *c* What Bohemian rebellions had there been and were Austrian suspicions that there might be 'a new revolt' (line 14) justified?

* *d* What events permitted Leopold to take such a harsh line against the Hungarian protestants? Was his policy successful?

## 3 Hungarian Concessions

I That all and singular the states and orders within that kingdom, whether they be peers, or gentlemen, or free cities and privileged towns, that immediately relate to the crown, shall remain in their faith and religion.

5 II That all the Hungarian soldiers that inhabit on the frontiers of the kingdom, shall enjoy the same freedom of religion.

III That not only the aforesaid liberty in religion shall be granted to them, but also the free use and exercise thereof, saving to the several lords of the soil their rights and properties.

10 IV That it shall not be lawful for either party hereafter to remove or expel the ministers of the church for religion. . . .

V That there shall be no more seizure of churches.

VI That those churches which, in the time of the late troubles, from 1670 till now, have been seized, shall remain to their present possessors.

15 VII That in every country, those of the Augustan [Protestant] confession . . . shall have liberty to build a church for the exercise of their religion, if there be none there already.

VIII That if they have any churches there already, they shall be left to them, together with the revenues thereunto belonging.

20 IX That it shall be lawful for the peers and gentlemen in the said countries to erect and endow chapels, or places of worship, for the exercise of their religions, within their respective castles.

X That all things contained in the first article of the pacification at Vienna, shall be in force.

25 XI That in all parts of the kingdom of Hungary belonging to the emperor, the catholicks shall have the free use and exercise of their religion.

XII That particularly those of Posnia, that are of the Augustan confession, shall have power to build one church . . . also that those of

30 the city of Sopronia shall remain undisturbed in the . . . exercise of their religion. . . .

XIII That the grievances which hereafter arise in matters of religion, shall not be determined by force of arms, but by the king alone, after he hath heard both parties. . . .

35 XIV That all the inhabitants of the kingdom, of what rank, order, or degree so ever, shall abstain from reviling and reproaching each others religion, or the professors thereof, upon pain of incurring his majesty's highest displeasure. . . .

It was [now] hoped that his imperial majesty, together with the states

40 of Hungary, and the princes and states in the Empire, would speedily
unite against the French, whom they now look upon as the common
enemy of Christendom rather than the Turk.

> 'The Emperor's Concession to his Protestant Subjects of
> Hungary', 1681, in *Somers Tracts*, vol VIII, London, 1812,
> pp 591—2

## Questions

* *a* What events led Leopold to make these concessions?
  *b* What solutions did this document propose for developing freedom of
  worship in Hungary?
* *c* Why did Leopold view the French 'as the common enemy of
  Christendom rather than the Turk' (lines 41—2)?
* *d* How successful were these concessions in winning Leopold support
  among the Hungarians?

## 4 The Turkish Declaration of War

You have for some time past acted to our prejudice, and violated our
Friendship, although we have not offended you, neither by War, or any
otherwise; but you have taken private advice with other Kings, and your
Council's how to take off your Yoke, in which you have acted very
5 Indiscreetly, and thereby have exposed your People to fear and danger,
having nothing to expect but Death, which you have brought upon
yourselves. For I declare unto you, I will make my self your Master,
pursue you from *East* to *West*, and extend my Majesty to the end of the
Earth; in all which you shall find my Power to your great prejudice. I
10 assure you that you shall feel the weight of my Power; and for that you
have put your hope and expectation in the strength of some Towns and
Castles, I have given command to overthrow them, and to trample under
feet with my Horses, all that is acceptable and pleasant in your Eyes,
leaving nothing hereafter by which you shall make a friendship with me,
15 or any fortified places to put your trust in: For I have resolved without
retarding of time, to ruin both you and your People, to take the *German*
Empire according to my pleasure, and to leave in the Empire a
Commemoration of my dreadful Sword, that it may appear to all, it will
be a pleasure to me, to give a publick establishment of my Religion, and
20 to pursue your Crucified God, whose Wrath I fear not, nor his coming to
your Assistance, to deliver you out of my hands. I will according to my
pleasure put your Sacred Priests to the Plough, and expose the Brests of
your Matrons to be Suckt by Dogs and other Beasts.

You will therefore do well to forsake your Religion, or else I will give
25 Order to Consume you with Fire. This is enough said unto you, and to
give you to understand what I would have, in case you have a mind to
know it.

Text from a London broadsheet, 1683, quoted in
C. A. Macartney, *The Habsburg and Hohenzollern Dynasties*,
Macmillan, 1970, p 58

## Questions

\*    *a*    In what ways had Austria 'violated' Turkish friendship by attempting
to remove her 'Yoke' (lines 1−4)?

\*    *b*    'You shall feel the weight of my Power' (line 10). How powerful was
the Ottoman 'Empire at this time?

\*    *c*    What 'fortified places' (line 15) did Austria rely on?

    *d*    What does this extract reveal of the Turkish attitude towards
Christianity?


## 5   The Siege of Vienna

After a Siege of Sixty days, accompanied with a Thousand Difficulties,
Sicknesses, Want of Provisions, and great Effusion of Blood, after a
Million of Cannon and Musquet Shot, Bombs, Granadoes, and all sorts of
Fire Works, which has changed the Face of the fairest and most
5   flourishing City in the World, disfigured and ruined most part of the best
Palaces of the same, and chiefly those of the Emperor . . . After a
Resistance so vigorous, and the Loss of so many brave Officers and
Souldiers,   whose   Valour   and   Bravery   deserve   Immortal
Glory . . . Heaven favourably heard the Prayers and Tears of a Cast-
10   down and Mournful People, and retorted the Terror on a powerful
Enemy, and drove him from the Walls of *Vienna*, who . . . had so
Vigorously attacked it with Two hundred thousand Men; and by endless
Workings, Trenchings, and Minings, reduced it almost to its last gasp.

    Count *Staremburgh*, who sustained this great Burden, assisted by so
15   many Gallant Officers, having given Notice to the Christian Army, by
Discharge of Musquets from the Tower of *St. Stephen*, of the Extremity
whereto the City was reduced, they discovered on the Twelfth of this
Month, early in the Morning, the Christian Troops marching down the
Neighbouring Mountains of *Kalemberg*, and heard continually the
20   Discharges of their Artillery against the *Turks*, who being advanced
thither, were fortified with Parapets of Earth and great Stones, to hinder
the Descent of the Christian Army. . . . The Vanguard of the Horse and
Foot, seconded by the Polish Horse, had a long Skirmish with the *Turks*,
disputing every Foot of Ground; but seeing themselves totally vanquished
25   by the Christian Forces, who had surmounted all the Difficulties of the
Mountains, and drawn down their Cannon in spite of them, they retired
Fighting, leaving to the Christians all their Camps full of Pavillions,
Tents, Barracks, and Eight Pieces of Cannon . . . and retreated towards
their Principal Camp. . . . The Christians being ravish'd with the
30   Victory, pursued them with so much heat, that they were not only forced

to leave their great Camps, but likewise all their others, flying towards *Hungary*; And it is certain, had not the Night come on, they had totally defeated and routed the *Ottoman Army*.

'A True and Exact Relation of the Raising of the Siege of Vienna and the Victory obtained over the Ottoman Army, The 12th of September, 1683', London, 1683', quoted in C. A. Macartney, *The Habsburg and Hohenzollern Dynasties,* Macmillan, 1970, pp 59–60

## Questions

a   State, in your own words, the way in which the siege of Vienna was raised.

*  b   'Seconded by the Polish Horse' (line 23). How important was the role of John Sobiesky of Poland in defeating the Turks?

*  c   Why was the emperor 'at once triumphant and humiliated' (Voltaire) by these events?

*  d   Did the victory at Vienna transform 'the capital from an outpost on a dangerous frontier into the heart of a secure civilisation' (Williams) or did the Turkish menace remain?

## 6   The Evils of the French

You desire assistance from us for the recovering your kingdoms. We do assure your majesty, that as soon as we heard of this severe turn of affairs, we were moved at it. . . . If your majesty had rather given credit to . . . [us] than the deceitful insinuations of the French, whose chief aim
5   was, by fomenting continual divisions between you and your people, to gain thereby an opportunity to insult the more securely over the rest of Christendom: And if your majesty had put a stop . . . to their many infractions of the peace, of which, by the treaty of Nimwegan, you are made the guarantee . . . you should have, in a great measure, quieted the
10  minds of your people, which were so much already exasperated through their aversion to our religion, and the public peace had been preserved. . . . But now we refer it to your majesty, to judge what condition we can be in to afford you any assistance, we being not only engaged in a war with the Turks, but finding ourselves at the same time
15  unjustly and barbarously attacked by the French. . . . And this ought not to be concealed, that the greatest injuries which have been done to our religion have flowed from no other than the French themselves; who not only esteem it lawful for them to make perfidious leagues with the sworn enemies of the holy cross, tending to the destruction both of us and the
20  whole Christian world, in order to the checking our endeavours, which were undertaken for the glory of God, and to stop those successes, which it hath pleased Almighty God to give us hitherto, but further, have heaped one treachery on another, even within the empire itself. The

cities . . . have been exhausted by excessive impositions . . .
25  plundered . . . burnt and erased. The palaces of princes . . . are now
burnt to the ground. The churches are robbed. . . . In short, it is become
a diversion to them, to commit all manner of insolences and cruelties in
many places, but chiefly in catholic countries, exceeding the cruelties of
the Turks themselves . . . it ought not to be imputed to us, if we
30  endeavour to procure, by a just war, that security to ourselves which we
could not hitherto obtain by so many treaties.

> 'A Letter written by the Emperor to James II, setting forth the
> true Occasion of his Fall, and the Treachery and Cruelty of the
> French', April, 1689, in *Somers Tracts*, vol x, London, 1813,
> pp 18–19

## Questions

a   Why does Leopold credit the French with contributing to James II's
downfall?
* b   What were the 'many infractions of the peace' (lines 7–8) made by
the French?
* c   Was it true that the Habsburgs had been attacked 'unjustly and
barbarously' (line 15) by the French? (See also section VII, extract 5.)
* d   What 'perfidious leagues with the sworn enemies of the holy cross'
(lines 18–19) had the French made?
e   What was the 'just war' referred to in line 30?

# VI Louis XIV and the Government of France

## Introduction

Lord Acton argued that Louis XIV gave France something it had long lacked: 'monarchy personified, with as much splendour, as much authority, as much ascendancy, as would fill the national imagination and satisfy national pride'. Certainly France wanted a return to order after the chaos of the Fronde. Hence the widespread support for a strong monarchy and the theory of Divine Right (extract 1). Indeed, was Louis' emblem of the Sun not so much a sign of his alleged 'arrogance' as a symbol of Apollo slaying the dragon of disunion and civil war? Louis had a definite concept of the *métier du roi* (extract 2), but some would argue it stemmed very much from France's past so that his reign was 'one of continuity rather than one of dramatic change' (Shennan). Louis was the epitome of the 'grand monarch': 'Every event in the royal life had to be considered and planned with the utmost gravity. It would ill become a godlike ruler to be touched by the ordinary emotions of common humanity' (Ashley). Versailles embodied this, although many contemporaries were critical of his brain-child for its extravagance, for its removal of the monarchy from Paris, and for what some saw as a deliberate attempt to reduce the nobility to mere dandies and fops (extract 3). Some historians echo these criticisms, but others believe Louis deserves more credit for his patronage and ask: Can Louis be described as the first 'co-citizen' of Europe in his support for not just French but European culture?

Versailles was the centre of a new, far more efficient bureaucratic machine (extract 4). Crucial to its development was Colbert, 'the incarnation of method' (Treasure), who was determined to increase the king's authority in the provinces and to set the French economy on a new footing (extract 5). Some historians question whether he merely made a bad system work and so perpetuated it, others query whether his achievements were limited because of the indifference of Louis. Indeed, were Louis' ministers 'mere creatures who expected to be no more' or were they really the power behind the throne? Some historians have tended to compare Louis to a twentieth-century dictator, others argue that 'for the French, their government was a constitutional government, and Louis in some ways was what contemporaries thought of as a constitutional king' (Hatton), and ask whether Louis can be considered absolute in view of the rights of individuals and groups, the financial restraints, the obligation to take counsel, and the other limitations inherent in French society?

Louis' personal rule has been heavily criticised for its intolerance in matters of religion. Some believe the Fronde caused Louis to be obsessed with unity ('One God, One King, One Law') so that he saw religious nonconformity as not only blasphemous but also treasonable, while others would attach the blame for his actions on others. The consequences are equally disputed. Did his attack on the unorthodox forms of catholicism help to disrupt and discredit the French church (extract 6)? Was the revocation of the Edict of Nantes, though welcomed at the time by most Frenchmen, a major blunder that destroyed the French economy and united his enemies against him, or have its effects been greatly exaggerated (extract 7)? What is clear is that Louis' policies – and his constant wars – cast doubts on the value of having the strong monarchy so desired in 1660 (extract 8).

*Further Reading*

Excellent introductions to the period can be found in W. E. Brown, *The First Bourbon Century in France*, University of London Press, 1971; J. Lough, *An Introduction to Seventeenth-Century France*, Longman, 1954; J. Stoye, *Europe Unfolding 1648–88*, Fontana, 1969; G. R. R. Treasure, *Seventeenth-Century France*, Murray, 2nd edn 1981; and relevant chapters of the *New Cambridge Modern History*, vols v and vi. Two recent excellent biographies of Louis are P. Erlanger, *Louis XIV*, Weidenfeld and Nicolson, 1970, and J. B. Wolf, *Louis XIV*, Gollancz, 1968, both of which quote extensively from Louis' own words and contemporary accounts. Other biographies worth looking at are M. Ashley, *Louis XIV and the Greatness of France*, English Universities Press, 1946; V. Cronin, *Louis XIV*, Collins, 1964; P. Goubert, *Louis XIV and Twenty Million Frenchmen*, Allen Lane, 1970; R. Hatton, *Louis XIV and his World*, Thames and Hudson, 1972; N. Mitford, *The Sun King*, Hamish Hamilton, 1966; and D. Ogg, *Louis XIV*, Home University Library, 1933. A useful pamphlet is R. Mousnier, *Louis XIV*, Historical Association, 1974, and there are interesting collections of articles in J. C. Rule, *Louis XIV: The Craft of Kingship*, University of Ohio and in J. B. Wolf, *Louis XIV: A Profile*, Macmillan, 1972. Some students might find the Sussex Tape on *Louis XIV and France in the Seventeenth Century* useful (published by E. P. Ltd., Wakefield). There are not many works on the other personalities of Louis' reign, but there is a short biography of *Colbert*, by G. Mongredien, Paris, 1964, and a readable biography of the much-maligned *Madame de Maintenon* by C. Haldane, Constable, 1970.

A good selection of documents are collected and translated in H. G. Judge, *Louis XIV*, Longman, 1965; and this is usefully supplemented by W. F. Church, *The Greatness of Louis XIV: Myth or Reality?*, Heath, 1959, which has collected and translated judgements on Louis' reign by historians. Also worth seeing is the collection of documents in O. and

P. Ranum, *The Century of Louis XIV*, Harper and Row, 1972. It is still worth reading Voltaire's *The Age of Louis XIV* (Everyman's Library), which gives a beautifully written and perceptive account of the reign, though obviously biased in Louis' favour. This can be contrasted with Saint-Simon's version of events in L. Norton, *Saint-Simon at Versailles*, Hamish Hamilton, 1958 (or the three-volume edition of the *Historical Memoirs of the Duc de Saint-Simon*, Hamish Hamilton, 1974). Saint-Simon's account is very biased against Louis because, among other reasons, he felt Louis had wronged the nobility in removing them from posts of political power.

# 1   The Divine Right of Kings

It is God who establishes kings . . . Princes act as the ministers of God and his lieutenants on earth. It is through them that He rules. . . . Hence we have seen that the royal throne is not that of a man, but the throne of God Himself. . . . It is apparent from this that the person of kings is sacred,
5   and to move against them is sacrilege. . . . Serving God and honouring kings are things united. St. Peter groups these two duties together: 'Fear God; Honour the king'. . . .

As their power comes from on high, kings should not believe that they are its masters and may do as they wish; they should use their power with
10   fear and restraint as something which has come to them from God, and for which God will demand an account. . . . God gave His power to kings only to guarantee the public welfare and uphold the people's interests. . . . Princes are gods and share somehow in divine independence . . . only God may judge over their judgements and their
15   persons. . . . The prince may correct himself when he knows he has done evil, but there is no remedy against the prince's authority other than his own authority. . . . Majesty is the image of the greatness of God in the prince . . . who is a public personage, because the whole state is in him; the will of the entire people is embodied in his will. . . .
20   What is there that a wise prince cannot achieve? Under him wars are successful, peace is established, justice reigns, religion flourishes, trade makes the realm rich, and the earth itself seems to bring forth fruit more readily.

J. B. Bossuet, *Politique tirée des propres paroles de l'Ecriture Sainte*, c. 1670, first published 1709

## Questions

a   Why does Bossuet, who was one of the ablest members of the French clergy and served as court preacher, believe 'serving God and honouring kings are things united' (lines 5–6)?
b   Does Bossuet place any limitations on the power of the king?

c  List, in your own words, the ways in which Bossuet claims the
   monarch is different from other people.
*  d  Bossuet points out the advantages of a 'wise prince' (lines 20–3).
   What events in France had shown the disadvantages of a weak
   monarchy?
*  e  'The spirit of faction, strife and rebellion . . . was transformed into a
   rivalry to serve the king' (Voltaire). What effect did the theory of
   divine right have on Louis XIV and on his subjects?


## 2  The Métier du Roi

Two things without doubt were absolutely necessary: very hard work on
my part, and a wise choice of persons capable of seconding it. . . . I laid a
rule on myself to work regularly twice every day, and for two or three
hours each time with different persons, without counting the hours
5   which I passed privately and alone, nor the time which I was able to give
on particular occasions to any special affairs that might arise. There was
no moment when I did not permit people to talk to me about them,
provided that they were urgent; with the exception of foreign ministers
who sometimes find too favourable moments in the familiarity allowed
10   to them, either to obtain or to discover something, and whom one should
not hear without being previously prepared.
   I cannot tell you what fruit I gathered immediately I had taken this
resolution. I felt myself, as it were, uplifted in thought and courage; I
found myself quite another man, and with joy reproached myself for
15   having been too long unaware of it. This first timidity, which a little self-
judgement always produces and which at the beginning gave me pain,
especially when I had to speak in public, disappeared in less than no time.
The only thing I felt then was that I was King and born to be one. . . . A
King, however skilful and enlightened be his ministers, cannot put his
20   own hand to the work without its effect being seen. Success, which is
agreeable in everything, even in the smallest matters, gratifies us in these
as well as in the greatest, and there is no satisfaction to equal that of noting
every day some progress in glorious and lofty enterprises, and in the
happiness of the people which has been planned and thought out by
25   oneself. All that is most necessary to this work is at the same time
agreeable; for, in a word, my son, it is to have one's eyes open to the
whole earth; to learn each hour the news concerning every province and
every nation, the secrets of every court, the mood and the weakness of
each Prince and of every foreign minister; to be well-informed on an
30   infinite number of matters about which we are supposed to know
nothing; to elicit from our subjects what they hide from us with the
greatest care; to discover the most remote opinions of our own courtiers
and the most hidden interests of those who come to us with quite contrary
professions. I do not know of any other pleasure we would not renounce
35   for that. . . .

I resolved at all costs to have no prime minister. . . . To effect this, it
was necessary to divide my confidence and the execution of my orders
without giving it entirely to one single person, applying these different
people to different spheres according to their diverse talents, which is
40  perhaps the first and greatest gift that Princes can possess. . . . I could,
doubtless, have discovered men of higher consideration, but not of
greater capacity than these three [Lionne, le Tellier, Colbert]; . . . to lay
bare to you all that was in my mind, it was not to my interest to choose
subjects of a more eminent quality. Before all else it was needful to
45  establish my own reputation, and to let the public know from the very
rank from which I chose them, that it was my intention not to share my
authority with them.

>J. Longnon, *A King's lessons in statecraft: Louis XIV. Letters to his
heirs*, trans. by H. Wilson, T. Fisher Unwin, 1914, pp 48–57

## Questions

a  'Govern! Let the politician be a servant, never a master. . . . If you
take the government into your own hands, you will do more in one
day than a minister cleverer than I in six months' (Mazarin). Can you
see the result of Mazarin's training in this passage?
b  List in your own words, the ways in which Louis enjoyed his role as
monarch.
* c  'I resolved at all costs to have no prime minister' (line 36). In what way
did Louis organise his central administration to avoid this, and did he
make a 'wise choice of persons' (line 2)?
* d  'It was not to my interest to choose subjects of a more eminent quality'
(lines 43–4). Why was Louis loath to share his authority with the
nobles, and how did he reduce their role in central and local
government?
* e  'He is content to know the surface of affairs without examining them
sufficiently, and prone therefore to be prejudiced by people whom he
trusts' (Spanheim, the Elector of Brandenburg's envoy). Is this or
Louis' version of his role the true one?

## 3  The Court at Versailles

(a) Versailles, that most dismal and thankless of spots, without vistas,
woods, or water, without soil, even, for all the surrounding land is
quicksand or bog, and the air cannot be healthy. . . . He [Louis] set up
one building after another according to no scheme of planning. Beauty
5  and ugliness, spaciousness and meanness were roughly tacked together.
The royal apartments at Versailles are beyond everything inconvenient,
with back-views over the privies and other dark and evil-smelling places.
Truly, the magnificence of the gardens is amazing, but to make the
smallest use of them is disagreeable, and they are in equally bad
10  taste. . . . But one might be for ever pointing out the monstrous defects

of that huge and immensely costly palace, and of its outhouses that cost even more. . . .

The frequent entertainments, the private drives at Versailles and the royal journeys, provided the King with a means of distinguishing or mortifying his courtiers by naming those who were or were not to accompany him, and thus keeping everyone eager and anxious to please him. He fully realised that the substantial gifts which he had to offer were too few to have any continuous effect, and he substituted imaginary favours that appealed to men's jealous natures, small distinctions which he was able, with extraordinary ingenuity, to grant or withhold every day and almost every hour. The hopes that courtiers built upon such flimsy favours and the importance which they attached to them was really unbelievable.

> Saint-Simon at Versailles, trans. by L. Norton, Hamish Hamilton,
> 1958, pp 262– 3, 253– 4

(b) Louis XIV was seventy-two when I was presented at Court; I was fourteen; it is the age of marvels and illusions. I was almost annihilated by the majesty of his person and by the splendour of his imposing mien. . . . Having recovered from my first timidity, I cast my eyes on this great King, whom I found to be much above what I had been told about him. Nothing so majestic had ever met my eyes, and, of all the men I have seen, he appeared to me the one most worthy to command. . . . His air of greatness communicated fear, and I saw the imprint of respect graven on all faces. One of his looks was a command which the habit of seeing the monarch enabled you to divine. Unfortunate as he was abroad, he maintained at home a most imposing etiquette. . . . He maintained with his courtiers the attitude and air of a king; the man seldom appeared. He had accustomed all those who surrounded him to a kind of worship, and it seemed natural to be at his feet.

> The Private Life of the Marshal Duke of Richelieu, trans. by F. S.
> Flint, P. Elek, 1958, pp 22– 3

## Questions

a   What reasons does Saint-Simon give for disliking Versailles?

* b   What were the 'imaginary favours' (lines 18– 19) Louis gave to his courtiers?

c   What does the second extract reveal of the courtiers' response to their King?

* d   'The place he designed for his magnificence to show what a great king can do' (Mme de Motteville). Was this the only reason for building Versailles?

e   'He had accustomed all those who surrounded him to a kind of worship' (lines 36– 7). Compare this with the views expressed in extract 1.

* f   'The establishment at Versailles was more important and had graver

consequences than any of Louis' wars or all of his wars put together'
(Lavisse). Is there any justification for this statement?

## 4 The Role of the Intendants

*In regard to the church*, the names and number of the bishoprics, the cities,
towns, villages and parishes subject to their ecclesiastical jurisdiction, their
temporal lordship, . . . the name, age, estate and attitude of each
bishop, . . . the influence he enjoys in the region and the effect he might
5 have in troublesome times. . . .
*In regard to military matters*, which concern the nobility, the second order
of the realm . . . the *maîtres des requêtes* should begin their investigation
by naming the Governor-generals, their family and connections in the
province, whether they are in residence at present, their good and bad
10 conduct, . . . how much influence they enjoy among the nobility and
people. . . . As for the ordinary nobility, it is good to know the number
and names of the most highly regarded, . . . whether many have gone to
war, whether they cultivate their own lands or rent them to
others. . . .
15 *As for judicial affairs*, the *maîtres des requêtes* must examine carefully the
members of any Parlement or other sovereign body in the
province. . . . They must examine its entire conduct during His
Majesty's minority. . . . It will be desirable, indeed essential, to know in
detail the interests and talents of their principal officers. . . .
20 *As for finances*, in those provinces having a *cour des aides* it will be good to
know the names of officials, their ability and their family
ties, . . . whether there is any manifest corruption among them, and full
details must be acquired of any scandals. . . . It remains to examine the
revenues of the King and allied matters. They consist of the domains,
25 which are all often alienated and therefore produce no revenue, the farms
of the *traites*, the *aides*, the *gabelle*, various other dues, and the *taille*. . . . It
is necessary to discover and punish the main abuses . . . [such as] the false
nobles and others exempt from taxation who enter parishes. . . .
*In regard to the state of the province*, . . . the commissioners should carefully
30 observe the character and spirit of the people in each province, each
region, and each town, whether they are inclined to war, agriculture,
industry or commerce; . . . whether there are many sailors of a good
reputation; whether the land is cultivated everywhere or not and whether
it is fertile; what crops it produces; whether the inhabitants are
35 industrious; . . . and what industry and trade is found. . . .
His Majesty will take care to know those [intendants] who have served
him best by reading the accounts they submit to him in his council, in
order that he may bestow on them marks of his satisfaction.
'Instruction pour les Maîtres des Requêtes, commissaires départis
dans les provinces', 1663/4, from *Lettres, instructions et mémoires de
Colbert*, ed. by P. Clément, Paris, 1867, vol IV, pp 27–43

## Questions

a  What were the *maîtres des requêtes* (line 7)?

b  'The intendant gives constant intelligence of all things to the court.' What evidence for this is provided by this extract?

*  c  What was the role of (i) the governor-general (line 8) (ii) the parlement (line 15) and (iii) the *cour des aides* (line 20)?

d  What thinking lay behind Louis' instructions about investigating (i) the nobility and their various functions, and (ii) the finances and the general state of each province?

*  e  What were 'the *traites*, the *aides*, the *gabelle* . . . and the *taille*' (line 26)?

*  f  'No officials of a government had wielded such powers since the time of the Roman Empire' (Treasure). Comment on the developing role of the intendants in Louis' reign.


## 5 Colbert and Economic Change

Your Majesty knows that his finances were reduced to twenty-three million livres in revenue [in 1661] . . . [but] within two years the amount increased to fifty-eight and then to seventy million livres in revenue. During nine years of great abundance, the general administration was
5   based on this income, and all expenditures which were beneficial to the state were made. . . . During the course of this year [1670] I find that the abundance, which could be seen everywhere, has disappeared for two very compelling reasons. . . . The first is the increase in expenditures, which are reaching seventy-five million, and which therefore exceed
10   revenues by five million in peacetime. The other is the problems which tax farmers and receivers-general are having in collecting money from the provinces . . and their daily protests that the great poverty they see will bring them financial ruin. . . .

I confess that when I first noticed it, my first thought was to cut back
15   the expenditures on the navy, buildings, commerce, and even debt repayments . . . in order to give priority to war expenditures and royal household expenditures . . . [but] I thought it was first necessary to share with Your Majesty all the information that I have gathered. . . .

We should have done one of two things to prevent this trouble: either
20   decrease taxes and expenditures or increase the amount of money in commerce. Regarding the first, taxes have been decreased; but . . . the *taille*, which used to produce sixteen million out of the fifty-six million estimated, now, on the basis of thirty-two million, produces twenty-four; and the *gabelle*, which used to produce only one million, at present
25   produces thirteen. . . . Regarding the second, . . . it was essential to introduce it into the realm, where neither the country nor individuals had ever given full attention to it, because commerce is contrary to the character of the nation to a certain degree. . . . All the commerce from

port to port, even within the realm, used to be carried on by the
30   Dutch . . . [but] we have seen the number of French vessels increase
yearly; and . . . Your Majesty ordered work done to abolish all the tolls
which had long been established on all rivers of the kingdom,
and . . . Your Majesty ordered the tariff of 1664, in which import duties
are regulated in a completely different way. All merchandise and
35   manufactured items of the realm were clearly favoured and the foreign
ones priced out of the market, though not completely, because, not yet
having established manufactures in the realm, an excessive increase in
duties would have been a great burden to the people. . . . This change
began to provide some means of establishing manufactures in the
40   realm. . . . But all these great things and countless others . . . are still in
their infancy and can be carried out to perfection only with more work
and effort, and can continue only if the state is flourishing. . . .
    It is certain, Sire, that Your Majesty, as king, and the greatest of all the
kings who has ever mounted upon the throne, prefers war over all other
45   things by his very nature, and that the administration of his finances and
everything which relates to it, and which consists of dull figures, is not the
normal, natural function of kings. Your Majesty thinks of war ten times
more than he thinks of his finances. . . . [But if war occurs] here are the
results which the present financial situation can bring: either it will oblige
50   us to begin using the revenues of coming years, or it will prevent the
continuation and execution of all the great plans explained in this
memorandum.

> 'Mémoire au Roi sur les finances', 1670, in *Lettres, Instructions et
> Mémoires de Colbert*, ed. by P. Clément, Paris, 1870, vol VII, pp
> 233–56

## Questions

* a  Why was crown expenditure increasing by the 1670s?
* b  How did Colbert manage to decrease some taxes yet increase the
     revenue of the king?
  c  Outline some of the changes Colbert made and which he mentions in
     this memorandum.
* d  Why did Colbert believe commerce was 'contrary to the character of
     the nation to a certain degree' (lines 27–8)? What did he try to do to
     alter this in the years 1660–85?
  e  What do you think Colbert is recommending Louis should
     do to improve the financial situation? What evidence is there
     in the memorandum that he knows Louis will not like his
     advice?
* f  'Colbert brought both knowledge and genius to the
     administration . . . there is little that was not either re-established or
     created in his time' (Voltaire). Comment.

# 6 Catholic Nonconformity

The Jesuits made themselves masters of the courts through the confessionals of almost every Catholic sovereign, and masters of the public by the instruction of children. . . . They made themselves pleasant by a smoothness and a charm never before encountered in penitential sessions,
5  and were especially favoured by Rome because of a fourth vow of obedience to the Pope, which is peculiar to their Society and most efficacious in extending papal supremacy. People revered them also for the austerity of their lives, devoted as they were to learning, the defence of the Church against heresy, and the sanctification of their
10  Society. . . . [They] risked the publication of a book by their own Père Molina, offering a doctrine on Grace utterly contrary to . . . the Church of Rome. . . . The Church of France, in particular, opposed [this as] a seductively novel theory that was gaining many adherents by offering easy salvation and appealing to human vanity. The Jesuits . . . succeeded
15  in turning the tables on their opponents by the invention of a new heresy [Jansenism]. . . . They thus became the accusers, not the defendants. . . .

At that time many saints and scholars lived in pious retirement at the Abbey of Port-Royal-des-Champs. . . . The greatest works on moral science, those universally acclaimed as shedding light on the principles
20  and practice of religion, were written by them. These learned men possessed friends and connections, who also entered the quarrel against Molinism, which was enough to turn the Jesuits' earlier suspicions to implacable hatred, ending in the persecution of the Jansenists of the Sorbonne, of M. Arnauld who was regarded as the leader of them all, and
25  finally in the dispersal of the hermits of Port-Royal. The next event in the dispute was a move by the Jesuits to introduce a formal statement of doctrine . . . by which the so-called heresy was not only proscribed . . . but was explicitly stated to occur in the book entitled 'Augustinus', by Cornelius Jansen. . . . The proscription of five heretical
30  propositions in which no one believed did not present the slightest difficulty; the statement as a tenet of faith that they were contained in Jansen's book created much, for not one of them could be found there. . . .

At the Court no effort was spared to assist the Jesuits . . . by spreading
35  a belief that the Jansenists were revolutionaries, as much opposed to the King's authority as they were to that of the Pope.

*Historical Memoirs of the Duc de Saint-Simon*, vol I, trans. by L. Norton, Hamish Hamilton, 1967, pp 491–3

## Questions

a  What is Saint-Simon's attitude towards the Jesuits? What reasons does he give for their political power?

*  b  Did the Jansenists come into conflict with the Jesuits over 'a doctrine

on Grace' (line 11), or were there other factors behind the controversy?

* c What problems arose out of the Jesuit attempt to introduce 'a formal statement of doctrine' (lines 26–7)? Why did this lead Louis at a later stage to abandon his Gallican policies and seek greater cooperation with the papacy?

* d 'He felt a personal sense of responsibility for the religious life of all his subjects' (Ashley). What attempts did Louis make to impose religious conformity on all his catholic subjects, and to resolve the Jansenist controversy?

## 7 The Revocation of the Edict of Nantes

(a) If this hydra that your hand has strangled
Does not provide to your *vertu* the worthiest of trophies
Then think of the cruel misfortunes that this sect has caused,
See how it has divided your subjects,
5  Consider in your heart its fatal practices.
How much blood poured forth, how many tragic stories of
The sacrileges of profaned altars,
Priests scorned and degraded, temples destroyed,
Blasphemies carried up to the sanctuary,
10 By all this see what it had been able to do.

To purge the state of an internal pestilence
Louis saw that it was time to cut its roots.
He broke the edicts by which our recent kings
Allowed this serpent the right to speak
15 From which never ceased to come its false maxims
Infecting minds and fomenting crimes.

> Le Clerc, *Le Triomphe de la Foy*, 1686, trans. by J. B. Wolf, *Louis XIV*, Gollancz, 1968, p 395

(b) The revocation of the Edict of Nantes, decided upon without the least excuse or any need, and the many proscriptions and declarations that followed it, was the outcome of a terrible plot which depopulated a
20 quarter of the kingdom; ruined its commerce; weakened all parties; caused widespread pillage and condoned the dragonnades; authorised the tortures and torments in which thousands of innocent people of both sexes died; tore apart families, kinsmen against kinsmen, in order to seize their property and let them die of hunger; caused our manufacturers to
25 emigrate so that foreign states flourished at the expense of ours; and gave to them the spectacle of such a remarkable a people being proscribed, stripped of their possessions, exiled, and forced to seek refuge far from their native land, without being guilty of any crime. . . . And to crown all these horrors it filled every province of the realm with perjurors and

30  sacrilegers . . . who dragged themselves to adore what they did not
believe in.

Saint-Simon, *La Cour de Louis XIV*, Paris, 1911, p 416

## Questions

*a*  What impression does Le Clerc give of the attitude of the Catholics to
Huguenots?

\*  *b*  What were the 'cruel misfortunes' (line 3) that the sect caused, or was
this a figment of the poet's imagination?

\*  *c*  What were (i) the 'edicts' (line 13) which Louis broke, and (ii) the
'dragonnades' (line 21)?

\*  *d*  'Decided upon without the least excuse or any need' (lines 17–18). Is
this a fairer assessment of Louis' action than that given by Le Clerc?

\*  *e*  List, in your own words, the results that, according to Saint-Simon,
revocation produced. How exaggerated is his view?

\*  *f*  Why did revocation fill France with 'perjurers and sacrilegers' (lines
29–30)?

\*  *g*  Comment on the view that 'Revocation was a gesture which satisfied
Louis' highly developed sense of the dramatic in kingship' (Stoye).

## 8  France in Slavery

Quality, distinction, merit and birth are things no longer known. The
Royal authority is mounted so high, that all distinctions vanish, all lights
are swallowed up: for in the elevation that monarch has attained to, all
human mortals are but the dust of his feet. . . . Formerly the State
5   entered everywhere, nought else was discussed of save the interests of the
State, of the needs of the State, of the preservation of the State, of the
service of the State; to speak so nowadays, would literally be accounted a
crime of high treason. The King has taken the place of the State. . . . At
the French Court there is now no other interest known than the King's
10  personal interest, that is to say, his grandeur and his glory: this is the idol
to which are sacrificed princes, grandees, the little, families, provinces,
cities, and generally all. . . .

Thus, it is not for the good of the State that these horrible exactions are
made. . . . [France] might have lived in perfect tranquillity, all the
15  powers of Europe that might give it any umbrage were brought low; the
thrones were possessed either by infant princes, or by sovereigns of
mean capacity, and of a calm, a peaceable humour, exempt from
ambition. . . . This money [taxation] is only employed in fostering and
serving the greatest self-love and the vastest pride that ever was. It is so
20  vast an abyss that it has swallowed up not only the wealth of the whole
kingdom, but that of all other States, if it could have seized it, as it
endeavoured to do. . . .

He fosters in his Court and about him a crowd of flatterers, that

enhance upon one another . . . he fills all Paris, all his palaces, and the
25 whole kingdom with his name and deeds . . . and all for having snapped
from a weak and minor prince three or four provinces: for having known
to take advantage of the divisions of the Empire and of the little union and
understanding that there is between its members, for having stripped a
poor duke, for having purchased several important places; for having
30 desolated half his own kingdom by the persecution of Calvinism. Thus,
you see what the greatness of Louis the Great amounts to, it is a self-love
of an immense greatness, and it is that enormous passion which devours so
many riches and to which so many sacrifices are made.

'The sighs of France in slavery breathing after liberty. Done out of
French', London, 1688–90, pamphlet 2

## Questions

a   What charges does the author of this pamphlet bring against the king?
b   The author of the pamphlet was probably Pierre Jurieu, a Huguenot
    exile. He believed that Louis' *absolutism* had degenerated into
    *despotism*. What is the difference between the two?
c   Compare this extract with extract 1. How do the two differ?
*  d   'The greatest self-love and the vastest pride that ever was' (line
    19). Is this a fair judgement on Louis' character?

# VII   Louis XIV and his Wars

## Introduction

Louis XIV is supposed to have died saying: 'I have been too fond of war'. It was certainly a view shared by many of his contemporaries (extract 1). Various motives have been suggested for his constant involvement in war — religion, commerce, power politics, and the search for security — but the most commonly held view still remains that they were primarily a search for personal *gloire*. Most historians have portrayed Louis as suffering from 'egomania', but, increasingly, this view is being challenged. For example, Wolf says in his biography of Louis: 'I was surprised to find myself seeing Louis as a man who frequently felt psychologically insecure . . . a man who had trouble trusting his decisions or believing in his actions. He was the king who sought advice of 'experts' whenever he could find them, and, unhappily, . . . [they] were often mistaken'. Is, therefore, the view of Louis as a kind of 'Christian Turk' largely a product of taking contemporary propaganda against him at face value?

Whatever their origin, the French fully supported Louis' early wars. Indeed, would Louis have been foolish to have ignored the opportunities offered to him by the weaknesses of his enemies? The War of Devolution (1667–8) not only revealed brilliant diplomacy, but the new-found strength of the French army being created by Louvois (extract 2), while the Dutch War (1672–8) was seen as an attempt to remove a dangerous enemy and trading rival (extract 3). However, given the advantages Louis had, it is surprising he did not achieve more. Why was this? Did his alleged 'glory-seeking' hinder the actual campaigning? Did he hope to achieve later by diplomacy more gains than he could achieve by conquest? Was the Spanish Succession issue clouding his judgements? His reunion policy, though strategically valuable, has been particularly criticised. Voltaire claimed that it 'estranged, despoiled or humiliated practically every prince in Europe; it was not surprising that nearly all united against him'. Although Louis published his own version of the reasons for the resulting War of the League of Augsburg (1688–97) (extract 4), Europe saw it primarily as a product of Louis' arrogance and ambition (extract 5). Ogg writes 'there could be neither peace nor security in Europe so long as Louis was king of France', but was that really true? Were not his enemies just as naturally aggressive as Louis?

The later wars placed France increasingly on the defensive, as the devastation of the Palatinate indicated so violently (extract 6). The War of the Spanish Succession (1700–13), which was arguably 'the most justifiable and least necessary of Louis' wars' (extract 7), served to convince Europe that Louis could not be trusted and France that Louis had outlived his usefulness. Criticism of the king mounted, although he still believed he served his country's interests (extract 8). Certainly the Treaty of Utrecht was a greater achievement, in view of France's condition, than Louis is usually given credit for. Yet, when Louis died, it is alleged he left behind him a government that required (but did not have) a hard-working monarch, a court that was totally remote from French life, a nobility that was incapable of political activity (yet laden with privileges), a church divided and discontented, a middle-class politically and economically frustrated, and a peasantry reduced to poverty by crippling taxes and the demands of war. If these criticisms are accepted, they pose a number of questions. Did this legacy contribute not only to the end of absolutism, but also to the end of the monarchy itself in 1789? Did Louis' wars occupy energies that were needed elsewhere? Is it true that 'if any Bourbon king could have avoided the total collapse of the *ancien regime*, it was only Louis XIV' (Judge)?

*Further Reading*
See the Further Reading list to section VI.


# I  The Corruption of the King

You might say that he was to the manner born, for he stood out like a king bee amid all that crowd of people because of his height, grace, and beauty (even in the tone of his voice), and because of his princely bearing which was better than good looks. . . . The King's intelligence was
5   below the average, but was very capable of improvement. He loved glory; he desired peace and good government. He was born prudent, temperate, secretive, master of his emotions and his tongue – can it be believed? – he was born good and just. God endowed him with all the makings of a good and perhaps even of a fairly great king. All the evil in
10  him came from without. . . .

His ministers, generals, mistresses, and courtiers learned soon after he became their master that glory, to him, was a foible rather than an ambition. They therefore flattered him to the top of his bent, and in doing so, spoiled him. Praise, or better, adulation, pleased him so much that the
15  most fulsome was welcome and the most servile even more delectable. They were the only road to his favour and those whom he liked owed his friendship to choosing their moments well and never ceasing in their attentions. That is what gave his ministers so much power, for they had endless opportunities of flattering his vanity, especially by suggesting that

20  he was the source of all their ideas and had taught them all that they
    knew. . . .
        Flattery fed the desire for military glory that sometimes tore him from
    his loves, which was how Louvois so easily involved him in major wars
    and persuaded him that he was a better leader and strategist than any of his
25  generals, a theory which those officers fostered in order to please him. All
    their praise he took with admirable complacency, and truly believed that
    he was what they said. Hence his liking for reviews . . . and his
    preference for sieges, where he could make cheap displays of courage, be
    forcibly restrained, and show his ability to endure fatigue and lack of
30  sleep. . . . He greatly enjoyed the sensation of being admired, as he rode
    along the lines, for his fine presence and princely bearing, his
    horsemanship, and other attainments. It was chiefly with talk of
    campaigns and soldiers that he entertained his mistresses and sometimes
    his courtiers. . . . He had a natural bent towards details and delighted in
35  busying himself with such petty matters as the uniforms, equipment,
    drill, and discipline of his troops. . . .
        It is therefore enough to make one weep to think of the wickedness of
    an education designed solely to suppress the virtue and intelligence of that
    prince, and the insidious poison of barefaced flattery which made him a
40  kind of god in the very heart of Christendom. His ministers with their
    cruel politics hemmed him in and made him drunk with power until he
    was utterly corrupted.
        L. Norton, *Saint-Simon at Versailles*, Hamish Hamilton, 1958, pp
    247–51

## Questions

a  What does Saint-Simon list as Louis' good points?
b  In what way did his courtiers and ministers make him 'drunk with
    power until he was utterly corrupted' (lines 41–2)?
c  Compare Saint-Simon's view of Louis' relationships with his minis-
    ters with that of Louis' own description in section VI, extract 2. Which
    do you think is the more accurate picture?
*  d  To what extent was 'soldiering' considered to be the normal function
    of kings?
*  e  What is Saint-Simon referring to when he speaks of Louis making
    'cheap displays of courage' (line 28) during his wars?
*  f  'Every king who loves glory loves the public weal' (Voltaire). Discuss.


## 2  The War of Devolution

Louis, relying rather on his troops than on his legal arguments, marched
to certain victory in Flanders. . . . Louvois, the new minister of war, had
made immense preparations for the campaign. Stores of every kind were
distributed along the frontier. Louvois was the first to introduce this

excellent system of victualling the army by means of storing-places; . . . whatever siege the king wished to undertake, to whichever side he wished to turn his arms, supplies of every kind were at hand. . . . Discipline, which was daily more strictly enforced by the resolute severity of the minister, kept all the officers firmly to their duty. The presence of a young king, the idol of his army, made the very hardship of this duty easy and dear to them. Military rank from that time took on an importance greater than that of birth. Services were taken account of, not ancestors, a thing practically unknown before. . . . The infantry, on whom fell the whole burden of war, now that the uselessness of lances was recognised, shared the rewards which the cavalry had formerly received. . . . This campaign, fought in the midst of affluence, and accompanied by such easy successes, seemed like the peaceful progress of a court. . . .

Such great success allied to such great ambition roused Europe from her slumber. . . . French Flanders had been conquered in three months, Franche-Comte in three weeks. The treaty between Holland, England and Sweden, to maintain the balance of power in Europe and restrict the ambition of Louis XIV, was proposed and concluded within five days. . . . Louis XIV was indignant that such a petty state as Holland should presume to limit his conquests and make herself the arbiter of kings; his indignation was not lessened by the fact that she was capable of doing so. This action of the United Provinces was an insult which he felt but which he had to swallow, and for which from that moment he meditated revenge.

> Voltaire, *The Age of Louis XIV*, 1751, trans. by M. P. Pollack, Dent (Everyman's Library), 1926, pp 79–80, 84–5

## Questions

* *a* Why did Louis rely on 'his troops' rather than on his 'legal arguments' (line 1) in the War of Devolution?
  *b* List, in your own words, the army improvements made by Louvois.
* *c* Was the War of Devolution really like 'the peaceful progress of a court' (lines 17–18)?
* *d* In what way was Europe 'roused from her slumber' (lines 19–20)? How important a role did the Dutch play in this?

## 3 Views on the Dutch War

### (a) The Dutch View

Sire,

After reflecting on the good disposition which your Majesty's predecessors have ever had towards this State we find it difficult to lend credence to the reports which are circulating to the effect that this State has become the object of the powerful armament which your Majesty has caused to be assembled within your kingdom. Nevertheless, in the light

of the information which reaches us from all sides and of the reported
speeches of your ministers in the royal and princely courts of their
residence, which seek to convey that this armament is against us alone, we
10 have purposed scrupulously to examine whether there has been in our
actions or conduct anything which might have induced your Majesty to
substitute dislike for the friendship with which hitherto you have been
pleased to honour us. Having found no such thing for which we could
accuse ourselves or of which your Majesty has made complaint, we have
15 been unable to persuade ourselves that the justice which governs the
actions of your reign could permit you to take arms against the oldest and
most faithful of your allies. . . . It is true, Sire, that for some time there
has not been perfect agreement touching navigation and commerce, but
we have deeply regretted this and have done what might legitimately be
20 desired of us in order to prevent and remove the difficulties. . . . And this
we are still ready to do, not only in this matter, but also in anything which
might convince your Majesty of the unqualified inclination we have to
render you the honour and deference which is due to your person and to
your high dignity. . . . For the rest, Sire, we do not believe it necessary
25 to justify the armament which we are assembling on land and sea . . . but
we wish to assure your Majesty that we take these measures without
intending to attack anyone . . . and that we will disarm with joy as soon
as it may please your Majesty to relieve us of the anxiety produced by
your arms, surrounding us on all sides. . . . We order Sieur de Groot our
30 Ambassador to seek for this purpose a special audience of your
Majesty. . . . It is for this reason that we add to this present letter nothing
further save to pray God, Sire, to crown your Majesty's reign with good
fortune and to bless your royal person with health and long life.
Your Majesty's most humble servants,
35 The States-General of the United Provinces of the Low Countries.
Letter from the States-General to Louis xiv, 10 December, 1671.

#### (b) The French View

When I learnt that the United Provinces were attempting to debauch my
allies and were soliciting the kings my relatives to enter into offensive
alliances against me, I wished to put myself in a state of defence and I have
raised some troops. But I allege I shall have more as spring approaches and
40 at that time I shall employ them as I judge most fitting to the good of my
State and to my glory.

Louis xiv's verbal reply, 4 January, 1672; from F. A. A. Mignet,
*Négociations rélatives à la succession d'Espagne sous Louis xiv*, vol iii,
pp 657–9, trans. by H. G. Judge, *Louis xiv*, Longman, 1965, pp
20–2

### Questions

*a* What evidence is there in the Dutch letter of their desire to conciliate
Louis, both in what they say and in the way they say it?

*b* How does Louis react to their letter?

* *c* Why do the Dutch describe themselves as 'the oldest and most faithful' of Louis' allies (lines 16—17)?

* *d* Why had there not been 'perfect agreement touching navigation and commerce' (line 18) between France and the United Provinces, and was this the reason for Louis' menacing attitude?

* *e* What accusations does Louis make against the Dutch, and is there any justification behind them? (See also extract 2, lines 21—9.)

* *f* What action did Louis consider to be 'most fitting to the good of my State and to my glory' (lines 40—1) in the spring of 1672?

## 4  Louis' Memorial to the German Emperor

Those who shall examin without passion . . . the conduct which His Majesty has taken from the beginning of the War of Hungary to the present time, will have great reason to wonder that he having always been advertised of the design which the Emperor had formed of a long time, to
5   attack France, as soon as he shall have made peace with the Turks, he should have deferred the preventing thereof even to this hour. . . .

It is very apparent that at the time when His Majesty might have taken advantage of the disturbance which the War of Hungary gave the Emperor, so as to have obliged the Court of Vienna and the Empire to
10   yield to him, by a definitive treaty, all the places which had been reunited to his Crown, in consequence of the Treaties of Munster and Nimweguen: and by this means put a stop to all occasions of misunderstanding between him and the Empire, His Majesty had rather acquiesce to a treaty of truce or suspension, than by his arms be the
15   occasion of diverting the princes and states of the Empire, from affording the Emperor those succors he stood in need of, in order to repel the forces of the Ottoman Empire: and that His Majesty . . . had preferred the general interest of Christendom, before the good of his own Crown, contenting himself to obtain that provisionally, which in prudence he
20   ought to have demanded for ever. . . .

His Majesty was willing to give fresh proofs of his moderation, . . . altho he understood the Imperial ministers employed all their diligence and endeavours in most of the courts of Germany, to incline the princes and states of the Empire to enter into new leagues
25   against France. That by the treaty made at Ausbourg [Augsburg], they had engaged a considerable number of the princes and states to subscribe this association. That in the Assembly of Nuremberg all kinds of artifices and suppositions were made use of, to bring all those into this league. . . . [Nevertheless His Majesty] had taken no other precautions
30   for maintaining his dominions from all the mischiefs preparing against them, than to fortifie his frontier places, so as to put a stop to the designs of his enemies. . . .

And as he has not undertaken the siege of Philipsburg, to open to

himself a way to attack the Empire; but only to make secure the entry into
35 his estates, from those who would raise new troubles, so he offers
moreover, in order to facilitate a treaty of peace, to demolish the
fortifications of the said city of Philipsburg, as soon as shall have reduced it
to his obedience, . . . and to surrender it to the Emperor with all its
dependencies, upon condition that he shall never fortifie it hereafter.
40 As for the Electorate of Cologne, His Majesty offers to withdraw his
troops from thence, as soon as the Pope, either by his own free will, or at
the request of the Emperor, shall have confirmed the postulation of the
Cardinal of Furstemberg. . . . His Majesty is also very willing . . . to put
an end to those differences which concern the succession in the Palatinate;
45 and he offers on the behalf of Monsieur, his only brother, and of Madam,
his sister-in-law, a disclaim of all the places, territories, and countries, as
well as the movables, ordnance and every other thing which ought yet to
be restored, satisfaction for the damages being made in mony. . . .
It is upon these conditions which are much more advantageous to the
50 Emperor and the Empire, than to His Majesty and to his Crown, that the
public tranquillity may be reestablished and made sure for ever. . . . But
in case of a too long delay, or of a refusal to accept hereof, he charges from
this present, all those mischiefs which the war may bring upon
Christendom, upon those who have forced him to resume his arms to
55 prevent their evil designs.
'The French King's Memorial to the Emperor of Germany',
London, 1688, in O. and P. Ranum, *The Century of Louis XIV*,
Harper & Row, 1972, pp 281–6

## Questions

* *a* What reasons does Louis give for his decision to go to war in 1688?
Are they the real reasons?
 *b* Why does he claim to have put 'the general interest of Christendom
before the good of his own Crown' (line 18)?
* *c* Was the League of Augsburg a 'league against France' (lines 24–5),
and, if so, why had it arisen?
* *d* 1678–88 has been called the 'classical age of French fortifications'.
How did Louis 'fortifie his frontier places' (line 31)?
 *e* What reasons does Louis give for (i) besieging Philipsburg (ii)
invading the Electorate of Cologne and (iii) attacking the Palatinate?
Are his solutions to the problems really 'more advantageous to the
Emperor' (lines 49–50) than to himself?
 *f* What does this extract tell you about Louis' political morality?

## 5 The German Emperor's Reply

It is known to the whole Christian world that when the Peace of
Numigen [Nymwegen], within a little after its conclusion, was by the

French King many wayes violated, and large countrys and provinces . . . were, under the new and strange pretences of re-unions
5 and dependencies and the like, torn away from the Roman Empire, . . . it was at last agreed in the year 1684 . . . that there should be a mutual cessation from all acts of hostility, to be inviolably observed for twenty years. . . . Yet behold now again that flame breaks out on a sudden which the French Court unwillingly cover'd over for a time. The
10 French seize on the Diocess of Cologne, invade the Palatinate, besiege Philipsburg, and without observing any law or article of the peace, or so much as the ancient manner of kings going to war one with another, the French King falls most unjustly upon the Emperor and the Empire, like one that had been long secretly a contriving it: and at last forsooth in his
15 smooth-tongued fashion, not when he denounced war, but when he had already begun it, he orders his fallacious Memorial to be presented to us. . . .

When His Sacred Majesty, the Emperor, read this infamous libel . . . he easily perswaded himself that it was quite contrary to the
20 sence of the Most Christian King, and therefore far from having been read or approv'd by him, . . . it was compil'd by some malicious French minister of state. . . . [How vain a suggestion it is] that His Imperial Majesty should have an intent to make war with France (when he has neither an army nor provisions at hand, nay when all his strong places,
25 cities and provinces, as the event shews, by too much trusting the King's word, are left in a manner destitute of souldiers, and of all kind of necessaries for defence, and his whole strength gone against the enemy of Christianity). . . . [Augsburg] only established some ancient agreements betwixt the Emperor and some of the circles of the Empire. . . . it tended
30 to the hurt of none, but only to that which is most innocent, and allowed by all law, their mutual defence . . . and therefore the mighty Crown of France did not need to be afraid of it. . . .

The twenty years' truce ought certainly to have been stood to. . . . Wherefore if there be any regard to justice in the Most Serene
35 K[ing] of France (as it is hop'd) His Imperial Majesty has good reason to believe and trust, that he will of himself chastise and correct the calumnies and slanders of this scandalous French print, will withdraw his unjust arms, restore dammages, bring back all into its primitive state, permit the Most Serene Prince Clement, long since legally confirm'd by His
40 Holiness, to enjoy quietly the Electorate and Arch-bishoprick of Cologne, and will remit the cause of the Prince Palatine to a competent court of judicature . . . and lastly, that he will suffer the peace which he sayes he wishes for, to be procured in the time, manner and order as it is set down in the truce.

45 But if he be not willing to do these things, none can then suppose there is any other cause for the French King thus to revive the war, than that the singular favor of the Divine Providence, and the wonderful defence it has afforded to the House of Austria, are things displeasing to him, or that he fears the great encrease and enlargement of that august family . . . or that

50  he has a desire to raise up agains the beaten and depressed Turks by
diverting our arms . . . [or] he thinks himself not oblig'd by any pacts or
covenants, but that he may break them at any time at his pleasure.
Whatever it is, the Most Glorious King of France shall not escape the
infamous mark of a perfidious prince that violates his faith. . . . The Most
55  High has thrown down and humbled the Turk . . . and He will also
throw down and humble the French violater of a league which should
have held sixteen years longer.

'The Emperor's Answer to the French King's Manifesto, Translated from the Latin', London, 1688, in O. and P. Ranum, *The
Century of Louis xiv*, Harper & Row, 1972, pp 286—95

## Questions

*a*  State, in your own words, the reasons the Emperor Leopold gives for
rejecting Louis' arguments.

*b*  What motives does the emperor see as lying behind Louis' actions?

*  *c*  What were the terms of the Peace of Nymwegen, and in what ways
had they been 'violated' (line 3) by Louis?

*  *d*  What were 'the new and strange pretences of re-unions and
dependencies' (lines 4—5), and why had Louis been able to carry them
out?

*e*  In what ways does Leopold suggest that Louis' conduct has not been
worthy of a monarch?

## 6   The Devastation of the Palatinate

The king had decided to lay waste the Palatinate. . . . His object was
rather to cut off the enemy's means of subsistence than to avenge himself
on the Elector Palatine. . . . In February 1689, an order was issued to the
army by Louis, signed by Louvois, to reduce the country to ashes. It was
5  in the heart of winter; the French generals could not but obey, and
accordingly announced to the citizens of all those flourishing and well-
ordered towns, to the inhabitants of the villages, and to the masters of
more than fifty castles, that they would have to leave their homes, which
were to be destroyed by fire and sword. Men, women, old people and
10  children departed in haste. Some went wandering about the countryside;
others sought refuge in neighbouring countries, while the soldiery, who
always carry out to the letter orders of exceptional severity and fail to
observe more merciful ones, burnt and sacked their country. They began
with Mannheim and Heidelberg, the seats of the Electors; their palaces as
15  well as the houses of common citizens were destroyed; their tombs were
opened by the rapacious soldiery, who thought to find treasures there;
and their ashes were scattered. For the second time this beautiful country
was ravaged by Louis xiv. . . . Europe was horror-struck. The officers
who executed the orders were ashamed to be the instruments of such

20    severity. They placed the responsibility on the Marquis de Louvois, who had become less humane through that hardening of sensibilities which a lengthy ministry produces. He had indeed advised this course, but Louis had been master enough not to agree to it. Had the king been a witness of the sight he would himself have extinguished the flames. Within the
25    precincts of his palace at Versailles and in the midst of pleasures, he signed the destruction of an entire country; and he saw in this order nothing but his own power and the unfortunate prerogative of war; but as an eye-witness he could have seen nothing but its horror. Nations who until then had only blamed his ambition while they admired it, now cried out
30    against his severity and even blamed his policy; for should his enemies invade his country as he had invaded his enemies', they would likewise burn his cities to the ground.

               Voltaire, *The Age of Louis XIV*, 1751, trans. by M. P. Pollack, Dent (Everyman's Library), 1926, pp 148−9

## Questions

*a*   Was there any reason why Louis might want to 'avenge himself on the Elector Palatine' (lines 2−3)?

*b*   'He saw . . . nothing but his own power and the unfortunate prerogative of war' (lines 26−7). Is the devastation described by Voltaire untypical of warfare at this period?

*c*   'For the second time this beautiful country was ravaged' (lines 17−18). When was the first time?

*d*   What does this extract tell you about (i) the relationship between Louis and Louvois (ii) the response of the French army to their orders and (iii) the changing attitude of Europe towards Louis?

*e*   Why was France on the defensive after 1688?

## 7   The Will or the Treaty?

It would be unnecessary to tell you in detail of the urgent entreaties with which he [the Spanish ambassador] sought to persuade me to accept this will, both for the good of all Europe in general, and of the Spanish monarchy in particular. . . . I have studied with the minutest attention
5   all the drawbacks and all the advantages of either abiding by the Treaty or accepting the will.

    In following the first course, I noted the advantage of uniting several important states to my Crown and of weakening a power traditionally hostile to my own. I considered the ties established with the King of
10   England and the States-General, and the aim of preserving the general peace by scrupulously executing the Partition Treaty. On the other hand, I had reason to think that the more my power was increased by the addition of the states assigned to my son, the more hindrances I should find to the execution of the treaty. The previous negotiations and the
15   present uncertainty of affairs have shown me this only too well. The King

of Spain's will added still more difficulties. For since the Archduke was
chosen in the event of my grandsons' refusing the succession, the
Emperor would have been even more reluctant to agree [to the Treaty],
and even if he had done so, since the Archduke's refusal would have
20   transferred the right of succession to the Duke of Savoy, the last would
have been recognised as legitimate heir to the monarchy by the whole
Spanish nation.

Thus in order to execute the treaty it would have been necessary to
conquer all the states dependent on the Crown of Spain, so as to distribute
25   them in accordance with the terms of partition. This decision would
necessarily entail a war whose end could not be foreseen. Nothing was
more contrary to the spirit of the treaty. On the other hand, I say that my
acceptance of the will could give no one cause for complaint, if my son is
willing to surrender his rights, as he is in fact doing, to the Duke of Anjou.
30   In this way all pretext for war is removed, for Europe will have no reason
to fear the engrossing of so many states under a single power; my own
strength will not be increased and things will remain as they have been for
so many years. It is consequently more to the advantage of Europe as a
whole, and even more in accordance with the purpose of the Partition
Treaty, to follow the settlement made by the late King of Spain.

Louis XIV to Comte de Briord, ambassador to the United
Provinces, November 1700, from *Lettres de Louis XIV*, ed.
P. Gaxotte, Paris, 1930, pp 127–31, trans. by G. W. Symcox
(Librairie Jules Tallandier)

## Questions

*  a   What were the terms of Carlos II's will (see also section III, extract 7)?
     What were the terms of the Partition Treaty?
   b   What arguments does Louis give for accepting Carlos' will rather
       than the treaty?
*  c   Why had 'previous negotiations' and 'present uncertainty' (lines 14–
       15) led Louis to suspect the Partition Treaty would not work?
*  d   If 'acceptance of the will could give no one cause for complaint' (line
       28), why did a war result?
*  e   Why has the War of the Spanish Succession been described as 'the
       most justifiable and least necessary' of Louis' wars?

## 8   The War of the Spanish Succession

### (a) The Lord's Prayer, 1709

Our Father that art at Versailles
Thy name is no longer hallowed
Thy kingdom is no longer so great
Thy will is no longer done either on earth or on sea.
5   Give us our daily bread which we can no longer obtain

Forgive our enemies who have beaten us,
And not our generals who have defeated us.
Do not fall into the temptations of the Maintenon
But deliver us from Chamillard.      Amen.

> Verse circulating around Versailles, quoted in C. Haldane,
> *Madame de Maintenon*, Constable, 1970, p 224

### (b) Louis' Plea to save the Fatherland, 1709

10 I have conducted this war with hauteur and pride worthy of this
kingdom. With the valour of my nobility and the zeal of my subjects, I
have succeeded in the enterprises that I have undertaken for the good of
the state. . . . I have considered proposals for peace and no one has done
more than I to secure it. . . . I can say that I have done violence to my
15 character . . . to procure promptly a peace for my subjects even at the
expense of my personal satisfaction and perhaps my *gloire* . . . but up to
now my most important enemies have sought only to distract me, and
have used every artifice . . . to deceive me as well as their own allies
whom they oblige to make the great expenditures demanded by their
20 unbridled ambitions. . . . I can no longer see any alternative to take,
other than to prepare to defend ourselves. To make them see that a united
France is greater than all the powers assembled by force and artifice to
overwhelm it. . . . The aid that I ask of you will oblige them to make a
peace honourable for us, lasting . . . and satisfactory to the princes of
25 Europe. This is the aim of my thoughts . . . the happiness and well-being
of my people has always been and will always be to the last moment of
my life, my most important and serious consideration.

> Public statement quoted in J. B. Wolf, *Louis XIV*, Gollancz, 1968,
> pp 564–5

## Questions

a  What do you think Louis' attitude would have been to the parody of
the Lord's Prayer? In what ways does he try to regain the support of
his people in his plea to save the Fatherland?

* b  Why could the French not obtain bread (line 5)? What peace proposals
did Louis study in 1709, and why was this at the expense of his
'personal satisfaction and perhaps my *gloire*' (line 16)?

* c  'Our generals who have defeated us' (line 7). How effective was the
war leadership of 1700–13 compared to that of the early wars?

* d  Who was Chamillard (line 9), and why was he seen as a particularly
bad influence?

* e  Did the 'unbridled ambitions' (line 20) of Louis' enemies really make a
continuation of war necessary in 1709? Did France's continued efforts
finally produce a peace in 1713 that was 'honourable' and 'lasting' and
'satisfactory to the princes of Europe' (lines 24–5)?

* f  Was 'the happiness and well-being' (line 25) of the French people
really Louis' main consideration?

# VIII  Sweden as a Great Power

## Introduction

Historians have suggested various factors for the rise of Sweden, such as the vitality of the Vasa dynasty, the efficiency of the administration, the development of natural resources, the comparative social harmony within Sweden, the stimulus given to her economy by war, and the contribution of foreigners attracted to a country where 'they get a title that do a service to the State'. But are these factors sufficient explanation? Was not Sweden essentially unsuited to play the role of a great power? What motivated the nation to extend its frontiers despite its limitations? Were Sweden's motives basically economic? Or religious? Or was the basic motive, as Professor Roberts argues, a search for security against her neighbours, a search that then led Sweden to seek new resources, which in turn produced the aggressiveness that so alarmed Europe? Gustavus Adolphus is obviously a key figure. The harmony at home was personified in his relationship with Oxenstierna (extract 1), and this 'Captaine of Kings, and the King of Captaines' not only reshaped Sweden internally, but transformed her position amongst her neighbours. However, his motives remain a mystery, especially over Sweden's involvement in the Thirty Years War (extract 2). Some historians see this as the real turning-point to great power status, and they emphasise the importance of the gains at Westphalia in giving Sweden the territories she needed later to conquer the Danish and Norwegian peninsula; while others, like Roberts, argue that if Gustavus had not entered the Thirty Years War, Sweden would have remained a great power able to cope with the later challenge of Russia.

The strain of war had serious effects on the domestic situation. 'As the branches expand, the tree withers at the roots', remarked one contemporary. By selling royal revenues for lump sums and by rewarding nobles with grants of common land, the Crown created both financial and social problems for itself. These culminated in the demand for a resumption of alienated lands and revenues in 1650 (extract 3), which some historians argue developed into a revolution against the narrow oligarchy of Council families that threatened to eclipse the Crown. As the demands of empire grew, the problems increased. Queen Christina alleged one of her motives for abdicating was her dislike of ruling over 'a nation of soldiers', while the period of gains that ended in

1660 turned Sweden into a 'subsidy-hunting power' (Roberts), because of the tremendous costs involved in defending her extended frontiers: 'Other nations make war because they are rich, Sweden because she is poor'. The disastrous war of 1675−9 convinced most of the nation that the country required a strong monarchy devoted to peace and reform, even if this meant a 'Reduction' (extract 4) and sacrificing the Council and the constitutional doctrines it traditionally championed. Charles XI thus developed 'absolutism within the law' (extract 5), but whether Sweden in his reign achieved 'an internal strength and an external prestige such as she had never known before' (Reuterholm) or whether the reign was merely 'a model for the conduct of a second-class power' (Roberts) is disputed. So too is whether Sweden gained any advantages from her empire (or the conquered provinces from Sweden). By 1700 foreign affairs once again dominated (extract 6) and Charles XII's reign poses a number of problems: Did he throw away Sweden's empire 'in unjustified gambles on the battlefield, or did he − by nearly superhuman efforts of willpower and leadership − prop up the already shaky structure of that empire and prolong its existence beyond normal expectation' (Hatton)? Did he deserve his 'war lord' image (extract 7) or did his death rob Sweden of her last chance to retain her great power status?

The Treaty of Nystadt in 1721 marked the end of a century of greatness:

> The glory of the Age is past and gone
> We to our former Nothingness are fated.

And yet was it in Sweden's interest to lose her empire? Had not the burden been too great? A great period of economic recovery and constitutional government was to follow.

## Further Reading

The best introduction is in F. D. Scott, *Sweden: The Nation's History*, University of Minnesota Press, 1977. Also recommended are: C. Hallendorf and A. Schuck, *A History of Sweden*, Cassell, 1929, and I. Andersson, *A History of Sweden*, Weidenfeld & Nicolson, 1955. There are a number of interesting articles in M. Roberts, *Essays in Swedish History*, Weidenfeld & Nicolson, 1967, and M. Roberts, *Sweden's Age of Greatness 1632−1718*, Macmillan, 1973; and a useful debate is contained in R. Hatton and S. Oakley, 'The Rise And Fall of Sweden, 1611−1721', in *European History 1500−1700*, Sussex Books, 1976. J. Lisk, *The Struggle for Supremacy in the Baltic 1600−1725*, University of London Press, 1967, is helpful not only on Sweden, but also on her rivals.

There are a number of good biographies on the period, including N. Ahnlund, *Gustav Adolph the Great*, Princeton University Press, 1940; M. Roberts, *Gustavus Adolphus: A History of Sweden 1611−32* (2 vols), Longman, 1953; M. Roberts, *Gustavus Adolphus and the Rise of Sweden*, English Universities Press, 1973 (especially recommended); G. Masson,

Queen Christina, Cardinal, 1974; M. Roberts, 'Charles XI', in *History*, June 1965; F. G. Bengtsson, *The Life of Charles XII*, Macmillan, 1960; R. Hatton, *Charles XII of Sweden*, Weidenfeld & Nicolson, 1968; and R. Hatton, *Charles XII*, Historical Association Pamphlet, 1974 (especially recommended).

Those interested in seeing further documents are referred to M. Roberts, *Sweden as a Great Power 1611–97*, Edward Arnold, 1968.

## 1 Gustavus Adolphus and Oxenstierna

Trusty and well-beloved, I greet you well. I have received your advice regarding next year's campaign: it says much for your fidelity to me and to the fatherland. . . . I wish there were others who could deal with our affairs with the same discretion, fidelity, and knowledge. . . . I would
5 rather trust my welfare to your zeal than to any other man's. . . . So far, God has vouchsafed us a measure of hard-won success: may He now grant us grace that our righteous cause may triumph and come to a good end . . . but though I have a good and righteous cause, the fortunes of war are as uncertain for us poor sinners as the life of man. And so I urge
10 and entreat you, for Christ's sake, not to lose heart if the issue be otherwise than we would have it. I know that I may rely upon you to take care of my memory, and to look after the welfare of my family. . . . For nearly twenty years I have fought my country's battle . . . and I have sought no other reward in this life than to do my duty in the state to which God hath
15 called me. If anything should happen to me, my family will become objects of compassion; for they are women, the mother a person of no judgement, the daughter still a young girl; likely to make a mess of things if they are given their head; in danger, if others gain an ascendancy over them. Natural affection forces these lines from my pen in order to prepare
20 you – as an instrument sent to me from God to light me through many a dark place – for what may happen: it is, in all the world, the care which weighs heaviest upon me. . . . I remain, for as long as I live, ever your gracious and affectionate Gustav Adolf.

> *Axel Oxenstiernas skrifter och brevvexling*, II, i, 669  70, trans. in M. Roberts, *Sweden as a Great Power 1611–97*, Edward Arnold, 1968, pp 16–17

### Questions

a What does this extract reveal of the relationship between Gustavus and Oxenstierna?
b Why does Gustavus feel it is up to Oxenstierna to carry out his work if he is killed?
* c What was Gustavus trying to achieve? Was he right in thinking he had achieved only 'a measure of hard-won success' (line 6)?
* d 'In every direction, in every sphere, whether civil or military,

domestic or foreign, the king and his minister initiated reforms and
made constructive plans' (Lisk). Discuss.

* e 'An instrument sent to me from God' (line 20). How important was
Oxenstierna's contribution to the development of Sweden as a great
power?


## 2  Motives for War

(a) I earnestly moved him [the Chancellor] to declare . . . what he
thought of his master's inclination and ends and what were those
occasions that might incline him to peace or war. He answered that all the
world did know . . . his King had just cause and fervent desire to have his
5  revenge of the Emperor . . . for the safetye of his owne kingdome, and in
requittal of the coloured invasions and ayds sent by the Emperor against
him, and for respect of the house of Meckelburgh so neare allyed to him,
whose destruction he could not well digest, and the oppression of his
unckle the Bishop of Bremen. . . . [And also] for the releife of the
10  Electoral Palatine, with which formerly the kings and crownes of Swede
had kept strict correspondence and were united by antient offices of love
above all other in Germanye. And particularly for the cause of the King of
Bohemia, for whom he was willing to expose his life and fortune. But
that it did not become the wisdome of his master to embrace so great a
15  quarrell alone, knowing his owne strength unable to oppose the whole
house of Austria and the Empire. . . . To enter into the generall
quarrell . . . without being assured by confederacye of a sufficient
ground to goe through the war and to be able to beare some check or
adversitye, he thought no friend would counsell or expect it from
20  him. . . .

(b) I have heard a report that the States of Sweden assembled in
Parliament have remonstrated that their kingdom is exhaust of men and
money, and that is true; that they have shorn themselves to aid their King
against his enemy, but that with the Emperor and Germany they have
25  neither quarrel nor interest; and therefore they desire to be excused to be
engaged in a new war. . . .

(c) I have resolved that the King of Swede did intend conquest and
enlargement of his dominion, but especially to be master of this sea, the
ports and trades therein, and from thence to rayse himselfe a revenew, to
30  maynteyne the one without charge of the crowne of Swede and to serve
him for subsidye in any other war, and in the meane tyme to entertayne
an opinion that he would in the end doe great matters for the common
cause, under which shadow he hath well done his owne business. . . . The King of Sweden is grown already too great, and there is
35  more cause to balance than to increase him.

*Letters relating to the Mission of Sir Thomas Roe to Gustavus Adolphus, 1629–30*, Camden Miscellany, vol VII, 1875, pp 60–2 and 65

## Questions

a  What were the Swedish motives for joining the war against Germany according to (i) Chancellor Oxenstierna and (ii) Sir Thomas Roe?

*  b  Are the reasons given by Oxenstierna justification for Sweden's involvement or was it true that it had 'neither quarrel nor interest' (line 25) with the emperor?

*  c  Why should Sweden be concerned about (i) 'the releife of the Electoral Palatine' (lines 9–10) and (ii) 'the cause of the King of Bohemia' (lines 12–13)?

*  d  Did Sweden acquire the support of the necessary 'confederacye' (line 17)?

*  e  Was Roe correct in believing Gustavus (i) wanted to be 'master' of the Baltic (lines 27–31) and (ii) had 'grown already too great' (line 34)?

*  f  Is it true that Gustavus' policy was largely just 'a reaction to external pressures' (Roberts)?


## 3  A Plea for the Recovery of Crown Lands

We, the undersigned Estates of the Realm . . . have cause especially to represent to your Majesty, in all humility, that during these last years of war the crown has been greatly weakened by the alienation of its lands, and its interests now require that those lands be restored to it in some
5   convenient and proper fashion. For if this is not done, we cannot see how your Majesty can maintain your royal state and authority, or how the government of the country . . . can retain its present shape and constitution . . . for we esteem your Majesty's royal power as the buttress of our liberties, the one being bound up in the other, and both
10  standing or falling together. . . .
    Although by the blessing of God we have conquered sundry vast territories for the Swedish . . . crown yet your Majesty from all this has little more gain than the mere names and titles of those conquered countries, but precious few of their lands and incomes. . . . Your Majesty
15  is dependent on a parcel of uncertain and newly-devised imposts which are displeasing to the people, and cannot be collected without the impoverishment of the lower Estates and the destruction of the poor. . . . The intention of the Estates of the Realm has never been that customs, excises, and other extraordinary war-aids should be regarded as
20  the kind of impost from which the crown's certain and determinate revenue should arise: they were granted solely to give aid and support to the crown in crises. . . . But now we find that not only have they become

the crown's sole and perpetual income . . . but also a means for turning
our liberty into a servitude. . . . What have we gained beyond the seas, if
25 we lose our liberty at home?

From the many supplications, complaints and grievances which the
commonalty daily bring forward, you will see into what an unheard-of
state of servitude they have declined since private persons took hold of the
country; for some treat their peasants ill, either by raising their dues, or by
30 imposing intolerable burdens of day-work upon them, or by
imprisonment, or threats, or evictions; until the poor peasant is utterly
ruined. And if any man should venture to complain of such usage, he will
hardly find a court or a judge to take him seriously, unless he should go to
your Majesty and the Supreme Courts: and to these the commonalty can
35 scarcely come. . . .

Yet in spite of all this we find that there are nonetheless some who urge
arguments on the opposite side. They say, for example, that under noble
management the land would be better cultivated than was ever known
before. Commonsense and daily experience prove the contrary; for it is
40 natural for a man to take better care of his own than of another's. . . . It is
to be wished that the good lords and gentlemen who are the present
possessors and occupiers of the crown lands should amend their ways in
these matters; bearing in mind that since it is contrary to law and
statute that the lands of the crown be occupied by private persons, they
45 have no prescriptive right on their side, and can hereafter claim no legal
title of possession, now that the Estates of the Realm have called
it in question.

> 'The Supplication of the Clergy, Burghers and Peasants concern-
> ing the recovery of Crown Lands, 1650', in *Handlingar til Konung
> Carl XI: tes historia*, x, 70–98, trans. in M. Roberts, *Sweden as a
> Great Power 1611–97*, Edward Arnold, 1968, pp 101–5

## Questions

* *a* Why had the crown been 'greatly weakened by the alienation of its
  lands' (line 3)?
  *b* State, in your own words, the problem and the remedy that this
  petition conveyed to the queen.
* *c* Is it true that Sweden gained little more than the 'mere names and
  titles' from her conquests (line 13)?
  *d* What objections does this petition make to the crown's methods of
  raising money?
* *e* Were the Swedes really in danger of losing their liberty, or is the
  picture of 'an unheard-of state of servitude' (lines 24–35)
  exaggerated?
* *f* Did this protest at the Diet of 1650 mark a social, financial, and
  constitutional crisis in the history of Sweden? What was Queen
  Christina's response to the pressures placed on her?

## 4  Reduction in the Eyes of a Victim

The ambitions and mutual jealousies which animated these parties [of the lower orders] thus had as their consequence the discrediting in the eyes of the King not only of the Chancellor, but also of the greater part of the Council; and in their place the lower order of persons won all the favours
5 they could ever have aspired to. . . . They wished to see their families established, and hence they sought every means to enrich themselves. . . . The principal means they employed to compass their ends was so to arrange things that all private property was involved in such uncertainty that no man could be sure of his most insignificant
10 possession, no matter whether he had acquired it by favour of former monarchs and the services of his ancestors, or by his own thriftiness and ingenuity, but that all was to depend upon the King's grace, and that no subject was to have such a title that the King was not able to deprive him of it with some show of legality, and give it away to whomsoever he
15 would. . . . In order to effect their purpose . . . they had recourse first to the implementation of the Reduction granted in 1655, as a forerunner of another which was to be even more extensive; and in 1673 had the inalienable lands immediately resumed by the crown. . . . For they argued that since the King's coffers were now empty by reason of the
20 lavish outpourings of former times, some means must be provided to ensure that the present King should have the wherewithal to reward his faithful servants. . . . Why, then, should we not go to work by methods which are still everyday practice in Turkey, where the Sultan treats his subjects as though they were leeches; which, once they are full, must spew
25 out the blood they have sucked in, and so be reduced to first principles — that is to being poor miserable slaves. . . . For in matters of politics, and where reasons of state are in question, honesty must give way to utility. No account need be taken of any objections which might be raised by the Clergy: they can be induced to avert their eyes by talk of 'the public
30 interest'; and . . . they can be encouraged to hope that by these means they may be able to safeguard their own property, which would otherwise be eaten up with taxes; and this delusion will serve also to lull the other Estates, so that they will gladly lend a hand to the task of hacking broad strips from somebody else's hide, provided they can keep
35 their own skin intact. As to the King, it could be of no consequence to him whether the old families were flourishing or not, since the true nobility consisted in innate virtue and ability, and not in birth. . . . These were indeed dangerous counsels . . . and they produced that general revolution which is now an accomplished fact [the Reduction of 1680]. It
40 has neither enriched nor advantaged anyone, either in general or in particular, in the same degree as it has inflicted hurt. That hurt we are now experiencing; and it will be many, many years before it can be repaired, if indeed it can ever be repaired at all.

Carl Bonde, *Anecdoter uti Sweriges historia,* trans. by M. Roberts, *Sweden as a Great Power 1611—97,* Edward Arnold, 1968, pp 131—3

## Questions

* *a* What was 'Reduction'? What form did it take in (i) 1655, (ii) 1673 and (iii) 1680?
  *b* State, in your own words, the causes of reduction according to this writer. Is this a correct explanation?
* *c* 'All was to depend upon the King's grace' (line 12). Was this the beginning of absolutism in Sweden?
* *d* Did the state benefit from the fact that 'true nobility consisted in innate virtue and ability, and not in birth' (lines 36−7) or is it true that 'the tradition of state service which had been maintained by the old nobility was largely lost' (Lisk) to the detriment of the administration?
* *e* Were the Swedes reduced to being 'poor miserable slaves' (line 26)? Compare this extract with extract 3, which states the advantages of reduction.

## 5   The Absolutism of Charles XI

(a) So favourable was the Conjuncture for the Advancement of the King's Authority that he scarce needed to ask whatever he desired: each Body of the States [Estates] striving which should outbid the other in their Concessions. The Nobility and Gentry, who universally depend on
5   the King, as not being able to subsist upon their own private Fortunes, without some Additional Office, were under a Necessity to comply with everything, rather than hazard their present Employments, or future Hopes of Advancement. . . . These Dispositions of the People . . . gave him an Opportunity to lay the Foundations of as Absolute a Sovereignty
10   as any Prince in Europe possesses.
     J. Robinson, *An Account of Sueden*, London, 1694, pp 41−2

(b) Although we can in certain cases be said to be above the law, in that we have the power and right to alter, declare or moderate the law when some evident reasonableness or indispensable necessity demands and permits it; yet without such cause, and in the ordinary processes
15   established by us, to make any alteration, or to esteem ourselves so above the law that we should not be willing to permit our subjects to enjoy and use it to their defence and security − that is something quite alien to our kingly office, and incompatible with our subjects' well-being.
     Charles XI, quoted in M. Roberts, 'Charles XI', in his *Essays in Swedish History*, Weidenfeld & Nicolson, 1967, p 245

## Questions

* *a* Why were the times 'so favourable . . . for the Advancement of the King's Authority' (lines 1−2)?
  *b* Does Robinson offer any reasons why the Estates in Sweden became 'little more than the loyal echo of the monarch's voice' (Roberts)?

    *c*  State, in your own words, Charles XI's view of his authority?

\*   *d*  Did Charles XI possess 'as Absolute a Sovereignty as any Prince in Europe' (lines 9– 10)? Why did some contemporaries refer to his government as 'a damned French system'?

\*   *e*  Did Charles XI's 'absolutism' make Sweden 'infinitely stronger and more prosperous than it had been in 1660' (Lisk)?


# 6   Contemporary Assessment of Sweden's Position

Gustavus and his successors employ'd first foreign officers and soldiers, especially English and German, to discipline and regulate the militia; and . . . the nation has improv'd their military knowledge to that perfection, that at this day the Swedish armies have no need of the
5  assistance of foreigners, unless it be to enlarge their number. . . . The kings of Gustavus's family enlarg'd the Kingdom of Sweden above one half, by annexing to it several fair and well-situated provinces . . . [ which act] as a barrier from the invasion of the Muscovites, and . . . cover the whole body of the kingdom, which
10  would otherwise be expos'd on the Danish side. . . . [It is not easy to see the worth] of Pomeren and the Dutchy of Bremen, which lie at a great distance from Sweden; and . . . [are] sever'd from it by the whole breadth of the Baltick, and very hard to be defended. For this reason, some have doubted whether these provinces are of any great importance
15  to the Crown of Sweden . . . [but] 'tis evident that as long as the Swedes are masters of Wismar, and have a firm footing in Pomeren, they need never fear an invasion from the German side: besides . . . they may be very serviceable for the attacking of Denmark on the side of Germany . . . The Swedes have already been twice masters of
20  Prussia . . . but this occasion'd so much envy, and rais'd so many enemies to Sweden, that they were oblig'd to quit that conquest. To conclude, we ought not to think always of conquest, or to be too eager in mastering countries that lie conveniently for us; because others may do the same by us. Besides, 'tis a vertue to keep well what we have got; for too large
25  conquests serve only to weaken the foundation of the state, as well as the nation itself. . . . Upon the whole, the Swedes can cover the body of their kingdom from the invasion of their enemies. . . .

It now remains to take a view of Sweden's neighbours, and consider what good or harm she may expect from 'em. . . . [Sweden used to
30  have] no reason to be apprehensive of being attack'd by the Muscovites, unless they [the Swedes] gave occasion to it themselves. . . . However, last summer we have seen the Muscovite, contrary to his solemn promise the year before, break suddenly with Sweden, and besiege Narva with a very numerous army, but the brave young King has so entirely defeated
35  him, that 'twill be scarce possible for him ever to make head to any prejudice of Sweden these many years, or indeed to recover the overthrow he has met with. On the other hand, the King of Sweden has

no desire to enlarge his conquests in Muscovy, since . . . the Muscovites differ altogether from Swedes, in their language, religion, and
40 customs. . . .

In former times the Swedes liv'd for the most part in a good understanding with Poland. The Muscovites, being their common enemy, oblig'd 'em to unite, and that so strictly, that when the ancient royal family was extinct, they sent to Sweden for a new king. But this
45 election . . . gave rise to a mortal hatred between 'em. . . . At last the difference was adjusted by a great effusion of blood in Poland . . . [and] there remain'd no reason against the perpetual friendship and union of these two nations. . . . But now we see the King of Poland begin an unjust and dishonourable war with the Swedes, without any
50 reason; . . . but the young martial King has so confounded all his designs, and so entirely routed his armies wherever he met 'em, that . . . Poland itself may be in danger of being over-run. . . .

The interest of Sweden, with respect to Germany, consists, in general, in the Empire's continuing in the same state that 'tis in now . . . [and] a
55 punctual observation of the Peace of Westphalia. . . . Among the Protestant princes and sovereignties, the Elector of Brandenburg, in particular, was much dissatisfied with that treaty of peace, by reason that to satisfie the Swedes part of Pomeren was adjudg'd to them, which . . . plants a powerful and dangerous enemy just by
60 him . . . [and] obliges him always to maintain a great number of troops, and to burden his people with heavy taxes. . . .

Sweden and Denmark could never come to an accommodation, to the infinite prejudice of both these states . . . [because] if these two nations could but live in a good understanding, they might not only be very
65 secure in the peninsula of Scandinavia, but likewise despise all the attacks of their enemies. But the Swedes complain that in former times the Danes always endeavoured to bring them under the Danish yoak. . . . [Fortunately] Denmark does not now border upon 'em [the Swedes] for so long a tract of ground as formerly; and 'tis now much
70 easier for 'em to oppose the irruptions of the Danes. But . . . the other Protestants of Europe will never suffer the Danes to undergo any considerable loss; for they are well pleas'd to see the two Northern Crowns divided. . . .

From the time of K[ing] Gustavus . . . Sweden has been in good terms
75 with France. . . . The arms of Sweden have been the greatest instrument in wasting the power of that house [of Austria], and throwing the ballance of Europe upon the French side. 'Tis very true that the Swedes had some assistance from France; but, at the same time, that kingdom thwarted their designs on several occasions, and watchfully oppos'd their
80 becoming great. . . . But now that France is arriv'd at so high a degree of power that it huffs all the states of Europe, and pretends to prescribe 'em laws, Sweden is oblig'd in consideration of the publick good, which consists in preserving the ballance of Europe, not to assist France in the vast designs that she forms every day. . . .

85　　The Dutch have pursu'd all expedients to oppose the growing power of
Sweden, lest the Swedish grandure should prove prejudicial to the
advancement of their trade. So that the present friendship between
Sweden and Holland is chiefly grounded on this foundation, that the
Swedes would not tamely see the Dutch ruin'd, because their maritime
90　　forces would be a considerable addition to another power . . . and that
the Dutch are equally oblig'd to prevent the King of Denmark having too
great advantages over Sweden.

> S. Pufendorf, *The Compleat History of Sweden, Faithfully Trans-
> lated from the Original High-Dutch and carefully continued down to this
> present year*, London, 1702, pp 610–23, quoted in O. and P.
> Ranum, *The Century of Louis XIV*, Harper & Row, 1972, pp 181–
> 93

## Questions

*   *a*   What were the 'several fair and well-situated provinces' (lines 7–8)
        acquired by Sweden in the seventeenth century?
    *b*   What, according to Pufendorf, were the advantages Sweden drew
        from her acquisitions?
*   *c*   'Too large conquests serve only to weaken the foundation of the state'
        (lines 24–5). Had Sweden in fact acquired too large an empire?
*   *d*   Why did Russia 'break suddenly with Sweden and besiege Narva'
        (line 33)? Was Pufendorf right in thinking the Russian threat had
        been dealt with for many years?
*   *e*   Why did the King of Poland 'begin an unjust and dishonourable war
        with the Swedes' (line 49)? Why was Charles XII so successful in
        routing the Poles?
*   *f*   Why was Sweden so concerned for 'a punctual observation of the
        Peace of Westphalia' (line 55)?
*   *g*   What are Pufendorf's views on the relations between Sweden and (i)
        Denmark (ii) France and (iii) Holland? Is his assessment an accurate
        one?

## 7　Charles XII and the Obsession with War

On what foundation stands the warrior's pride,
How just his hopes let Swedish Charles decide;
A frame of adamant, a soul of fire,
No dangers fright him, and no labours tire;
5  O'er love, o'er fear, extends his wide domain,
Unconquer'd lord of pleasure and of pain;
No joys to him pacific sceptres yield,
War sounds the trump, he rushes to the field;
Behold surrounding kings their powr's combine,
10  And one capitulate, and one resign;

Peace courts his hand, but spreads her charms in vain,
'Think nothing gain'd', he cries,'till nought remain,
On Moscow's walls till Gothic standards fly,
And all be mine beneath the Polar sky.
15  The march begins in military state,
And nations on his eye suspended wait;
Stern Famine guards the solitary coast,
And Winter barricades the realms of Frost;
He comes, nor want nor cold his course delay,—
20  Hide, blushing Glory, hide Pultava's day:
The vanquish'd hero leaves his broken bands,
And shows his miseries in distant lands;
Condemn'd a needy supplicant to wait,
While ladies interpose, and slaves debate.
25  But did not chance at length her error mend?
Did not subverted empire mark his end?
Did rival monarchs give the fatal wound?
Or hostile millions press him to the ground?
His fall was destined to a barren strand,
30  A petty fortress and a dubious hand;
He left the name, at which the world grew pale,
To point a moral, or adorn a tale.

Samuel Johnson, *The Vanity of Human Wishes*, 1749

## Questions

a   In what ways does this poem reflect the traditional view of Charles XII as a man obsessed with warfare?

*   b   In what ways did 'surrounding kings their powr's combine' (line 9)?

*   c   'Peace courts his hand . . . in vain' (line 11). Was Charles' refusal to compromise with his enemies a vital factor in Sweden's decline?

*   d   What was the significance of 'Pultava's day' (line 20)?

*   e   'His fall was destined to . . . a dubious hand' (lines 29–30). What controversy surrounds the death of Charles XII?

*   f   What 'moral' (line 32) was usually drawn from the career of Charles XII? Would it be fair to say he was 'stripped of everything except his glory' (Voltaire)?

# IX  Peter the Great and the Emergence of Russia

## Introduction

'Apart from the Church, Russia had evolved none of those checks on royal power which restrained the most ambitious of western rulers . . . the peasants of Russia were increasingly having the shackles of serfdom clamped upon them. Moreover, the nobility had not managed to create national or even local Estates capable of standing up to the tsars' (Williams). The tsar was God's anointed, and, though he lacked an orderly system of government, being content to delegate the adminis-tration of a given sphere to a trusted person, he 'wielded absolute autocratic power' (Platonov). The 'Time of Troubles' had almost destroyed the Muscovite state and most Russians looked to the new Romanov dynasty to preserve their national way of life. However, national security required the development of an efficient army and a more organised state, which in turn required involvement with the rest of Europe. Tsar Alexei tried to steer a course between Muscovite tradition and Western innovation, but his son, Peter, recognising the contempt felt for Russian 'barbarism' (extract 1), had no qualms about 'joining' Western Europe to a much greater degree. To what extent the work of this 'human dynamo' (Raeff) can therefore be seen as a continuation of Muscovite policies is debatable, and historians question whether he was the sole creator of a new Russia, or whether he merely developed Muscovite policy, relying on the support of many individuals because 'the seeds of reform had already existed in the minds of the best men' (Pypin) (extract 2).

Most contemporary Russians believed Peter the Great's actions were 'shaking the very foundations of Church and State' (Shmurlo), and rebellions against 'the Antichrist', 'the Bloodsucker', were common (extract 3). In contrast, Europeans were impressed by the 'Tsar Transformer' (extract 4), even if they found his personal habits barbaric. For the historian Peter's reign poses many problems. 'The reform was at the same time natural and personal, deep and superficial, simple and complex, a single block and a mosaic' (Miliukov). Order and defence were high on his priorities (extract 5), so, was his aim only 'to triumph at all cost over the difficulties his warlike enterprises had created for him' (Miliukov)? His foreign policy was very successful, so, were the social and economic changes just by-products of his wars and diplomacy? Or did he wish to transform Russia so that 'no one can claim a place of higher significance in the history of civilisation' (Soloviev)? Did his administrative changes destroy the essentially personal character of Muscovite rule and give his successors a bureaucratic system that they dared not change, yet which proved increasingly unequal to its task? Did he 'decapitate' the Church, turning it into a mere government department, or did he simply seek to give it 'a field of activity more appropriate to its character' (Soloviev)? Did he create a genuine acceptance of western ideas among his nobility and thereby create 'two nations' because the peasants remained in their Muscovite past? Was contemporary opposition to his work a response to the reforms themselves, or to 'the militant character of his activity, the needless cruelties, the coercion and severity of his measures' (Platonov)? Were his attempts to change Russian dress and appearance 'trifles better left to hairdressers and tailors' (Kliucheusky) or an attempt to disperse 'the darkness of ignorance' (Byelinsky)? Were the reforms only superficial and his achievements 'not very great' (Sumner) or did they begin a process of 'modernization' which, after long delays, culminated in the Russian Revolution of 1917? Did he provide his country with an entirely new spirit (extract 6) or did he have 'no clear vision of a march of history irresistibly impelling Russia in a particular direction' (Anderson) (extract 7).

Peter the Great poses one of the most interesting questions in historical study: can one man change the entire destiny of a nation?

*Further Reading*

Good introductions to the period can be found in B. Pares, *History of Russia*, Cape, rev. edn 1965; J. D. Clarkson, *A History of Russia from the Ninth Century*, Longman, 1962; and the relevant chapters of E. N. Williams, *The Ancien Regime in Europe*, Bodley Head, 1970. The best book on Peter's predecessors is G. Vernadsky, *The Tsardom of Moscow, 1547–1682*, Yale University Press, 1969 (2 vols). There are many biographies of Peter. Strongly recommended are M. S. Anderson, *Peter the Great*, Thames and Hudson, 1978; V. Klyuchevsky, *Peter the Great*, Macmillan, 1958; and B. H. Sumner, *Peter the Great and the Emergence of Russia*, English Universities Press, 1950. There is an excellent collection of articles, many of them by Russian historians, in M. Raeff, *Peter the Great: Reformer or Revolutionary?*, D. C. Heath, 1963; and also worth looking at are M. S. Anderson, *Peter the Great*, Historical Association Pamphlet, 1971, and I. Grey, *Peter the Great, Emperor of All Russia*, Hodder & Stoughton, 1962. Those interested in his foreign policy should also see J. Lisk, *The Struggle for Supremacy in the Baltic 1600–1725*, London University Press, 1967.

# 1 The Barbarity of the Russians

The whole Russian race is rather in a state of slavery than of freedom. All, no matter what their rank may be, without any respect of persons, are oppressed with the harshest slavery. Those that are admitted to the dignity of the privy council, assume the lofty name of magnates, . . . have merely more splendid bonds of slavery; they are chained in golden fetters. . . . The people are rude of letters, and wanting in that virtuous discipline by which the mind is cultivated. . . . Devoid of honest education, they esteem deceit to be the height of wisdom. They have no shame of lying, no blush for a detected fraud. . . . Vice itself obtains the reputation of virtue. . . . Among such a quantity of tares some wholesome plants do grow; and the rose that struggles into blossom among this rank crop of fetid leeks, blushes all the more fair. . . . [Most Russians] are of an incult, slow, and stupid disposition. . . . They despise liberal arts as useless torments of youth, they prohibit philosophy, and they have often publicly outraged astronomy with the opprobrious name of magic. . . .

The Czar is endeavouring, by means of various arts and sciences, to frame a better state of things in his kingdom. If success should crown the prudent efforts of good counsel, people shall shortly be astonished at the fair edifice that will stand where there was nothing but huts before; unless some misfortune should happen or a defection of the people. . . .

For in former times the Muscovites obeyed their sovereign less like subjects than bought slaves, looking upon him more in the light of a god than a sovereign. . . . Sedition was almost utterly unknown in Muscovy of old; now you would think the rebellions must be chained one to another. Hydra's head did not sprout faster than fresh rebellions spring out of the very graves of traitors. . . . Is it the iron age [of Peter] that has banished olden fidelity and affection, and reverence for their sovereign, even from among the dregs of the populace?

J. G. Korb, Secretary of the Imperial Mission Extraordinary, *A Compendious and Accurate Description of Muscovite Affairs*, 1698, trans. in Count Mac Donnell, *Diary of an Austrian Secretary of Legation*, vol II, London, 1863, pp 192–6, 154–6

## Questions

  *a*  Why does the writer believe the Russian people to be barbarous?
*  *b*  This writer says that the Russians were 'in a state of slavery' (line 1), but a seventeenth-century decree stated: 'In our state of Muscovy, the serving men of every grade serve . . . and no one owns land for nothing'. What was the real nature of the 'service-state' in Russia?
*  *c*  What 'fair edifice' (line 20) did Peter build? What was its purpose?
*  *d*  Was Peter the Great responsible for banishing 'olden fidelity . . . and reverence for their sovereign' (line 28)?

## 2  Peter and his People

I well know that the favour I am obliged to grant them [the foreigners] publicly does not please all my subjects: but I have two kinds of subjects; I

have intelligent and well-meaning ones, who see plainly that if I
endeavour to retain foreigners in my dominions, it is only for the
5  instruction of my people, and consequently the good of the empire: I
have others who have neither sufficient discernment to perceive my good
intentions, nor candour to acknowledge, and cheerfully to comply with
them; who, in short, from want of reflection, despite all that appears new,
feel regret on seeing us emerge from our ancient state of sloth and
10  barbarism, and would hold us down, if it were in their power. Let them
reflect a little what we were before I had acquired knowledge in foreign
countries and had invited well-informed men to may dominions: let
them consider how I should have succeeded in my enterprises, and made
head against the powerful enemies I have had to encounter, without their
15  assistance!

I am represented as a cruel tyrant: this is the opinion foreign nations have
formed of me; but how can they judge! They do not know the
circumstances I was in at the beginning of my reign; how many people
opposed my designs, counteracted my most useful projects, and obliged
20  me to be severe: but I never treated any one cruelly, nor ever gave proofs
of tyranny. On the contrary, I have always asked the assistance of such of
my subjects as have shown marks of intelligence and patriotism.
 Staehlin, *Original Anecdotes of Peter the Great*, London, 1788, pp
 74—5, 292—3

## Questions

*  a  Why did Peter need foreigners for 'the instruction of my people, and
consequently the good of my empire' (line 5), and why did this
displease most of his subjects?
   b  What is Peter's view of those who oppose his actions?
*  c  What were the 'circumstances' (line 18) at the beginning of his reign
that obliged him 'to be severe' (line 20)?
*  d  Is it true that Peter 'fought barbarism with barbarism' (Khrushchev)
or did he never give 'proofs of tyranny' (lines 20—1)? (See also extract 3.)
*  e  Peter is often accused of dividing his country into two 'nations' but
this extract suggests a division already existed. Why was Russian
society so divided, and what consequences did Peter's reign have?

## 3  The Revolt of the Streltsey

General Schachin instituted an inquiry, by way of torture, touching the
causes, the objects, the instigators, the chiefs, and the accomplices of this
perilous and impious machination. . . . The torture that was applied was
of unexampled inhumanity. Scourged most savagely with the cat, if that
5  had not the effect of breaking their stubborn silence, fire was applied to

their backs, all gory and streaming, in order that, by slowly roasting the skin and tender flesh, the sharp pangs might penetrate through the very marrow of their bones. . . .

One of them detailed the following particulars of this most perverse plot. . . . [He said] that they had the intention to set fire, sack and ruin the whole German suburb, and when all the Germans, without exception, had been got rid of by massacre, to enter Moscow by force, to murder all that would make resistance . . . [and] to inflict death upon some of the Boyars, exile upon others, and to drag them all down from their offices and dignities, in order the more easily to conciliate to themselves the sympathies of the masses. . . . That when they had got possession of authority they meant to scatter papers among the public, to assure the people that the Czar's majesty, who had gone abroad, in consequence of the pernicious advice of the Germans, had died beyond the seas . . . [and] that Princess Sophia Alexiowna was to be raised to the throne until the Czarewicz should have attained his majority. . . .

General Schachin had the sentence that was drawn up against them promulgated and executed. Numbers were condemned to be hanged and gibbeted; many laid their heads upon the fatal block and died by the axe; many were reserved to certain vengeance. . . . How sharp was the pain, how great the indignation to which the Czar's Majesty was mightily moved, when he knew of the rebellion of the Strelitz. . . . Fervid as was this curiosity of rambling abroad, it was, nevertheless, speedily extinguished on the announcement of the troubles that had broken out in the bowels of his realm . . . [and] he took the quick post [to Moscow] . . . and began to cogitate about a fresh investigation. The rebels that were kept in custody . . . [were put] to fresh tortures. . . . As many as there were accused there were knouts and every inquisitor was a butcher. . . . [Peter himself] put the interrogatories, he examined the criminals, he urged those that were not confessing, he ordered . . . more cruel tortures. . . . The whole month of October was spent in butchering the backs of the culprits with knout and with flames . . . or else they were broken upon the wheel, or driven to the gibbet, or slain with the axe.

> J. G. Korb, Secretary of the Imperial Mission Extraordinary, *A Compendious Description of the Perilous Revolt of the Strelitz in Muscovy*, 1698, trans. in Count Mac Donnell, *Diary of an Austrian Secretary of Legation*, vol II, London, 1863, pp 80–7

## Questions

a  Who were the Streltsey, and what motives lay behind their rebellion?
* b  What was the 'German suburb' (line 11) and why was it disliked?
* c  For what purpose had Peter 'gone abroad' (line 18)?
d  'The bloody orgies revealed the pathological blemish in his character . . . [he was] violent and unstable' (Maland). What does this extract tell you about the nature of Peter's rule?

*   e   Did Peter's destruction of the Streltsey mark the time he became true
        master of his country, and so enable him to set about the task of
        reforming?

## 4   The Admiration of Europe

Everyone marvelled at the Czar's insatiable curiosity about everything
that had any bearing on his views of government, commerce, education,
police methods, etc. His interests embraced each detail capable of
practical application, and overlooked nothing. His intelligence was most
5   marked; in his appreciation of merit, or the reverse, he showed great
perception and a most lively understanding, everywhere displaying
extensive knowledge, and a logical flow of ideas. In character he was an
extraordinary combination: he assumed majesty at its most regal, most
fastidious, most unbending; yet, once his supremacy had been granted,
10  his demeanour was infinitely gracious and full of discriminating courtesy.
Everywhere and at all times he was the master, but with degrees of
familiarity according to a person's rank. He had a friendly approach,
which one associated with lack of culture. Thus his manners were rough,
even violent, his wishes unpredictable, brooking no delay, or the very
15  least opposition. His table manners were unseemly, and those of his staff
still less elegant. He was determined to be free and independent in all that
he wished to do or see, without the slightest regard for the comfort or
convenience of others. His dislike of being recognised was such that he
frequently chose to use hired coaches . . . or the first vehicle that came to
20  hand, no matter to whom it belonged. Mme de Matignon discovered this
to her cost when she went to gape at him, for he took her coach out to
Boulogne and other country places, and left her stranded, much disgusted
at having to return home on foot. . . .
One might go on for ever expatiating on this truly great man and
25  emperor, with his remarkable character and wide range of extraordinary
talents. They will make him a monarch worthy of profound admiration
for countless years, despite the severe handicaps of his own and his
country's lack of culture and civilisation.

> *Historical Memoirs of the Duc de Saint-Simon*, vol III, trans. by L.
> Norton, Hamish Hamilton, 1972, pp 122–3, 130

### Questions

a   What does this extract tell you about (i) the character of Peter and (ii)
    western attitudes to Russia?
*   b   'His interests embraced each detail capable of practical application'
        (lines 3–4). Why has Peter been called 'the Artisan Tsar'?
*   c   According to legend, Peter said: 'We need Europe for a few decades,

later on we must turn our back on it'. What was the purpose of Peter's Grand Embassy abroad?

* d 'A monarch worthy of profound admiration for countless years' (lines 26–7). How have historical attitudes towards Peter changed in the last 250 years?


## 5 Father and Son: The Importance of War

But, when considering this joy granted by God to our country, I think on the line of succession, a bitterness almost equal to my joy consumes me, seeing you unfit for the handling of state affairs . . . ; worst of all, you wish to hear nothing of military matters, through which we have come
5 from darkness into light, and while before we were not known in the world, now we are respected. I do not teach that you should be eager to fight without cause, but to love this subject and in every way possible to further and learn it, because this is one of the two factors essential in governing, namely, order and defence. . . . You give weakness of health
10 as your excuse for not being able to endure military hardships. But that is not the reason! For I do not desire labours, but willingness, which no illness can prevent. . . .

Considering with grief and seeing that in no way can I incline you to good work, I have written this last testament to you, deciding to wait yet
15 a little to see whether *without hypocrisy* you will change. If not, then know that I will cut you off wholly from the succession like a gangrenous growth, and do not imagine that because you are my only son I write this merely to frighten; in truth by the will of God I will do it, for as I have not spared and do not spare myself for my country and my people, how
20 should I spare you who are useless? Better a worthy stranger than an unworthy son!

Peter the Great, 'A Declaration to my Son', 1715, in N. Ustryalov, *History of the Reign of Peter the Great*, St Petersburg, 1858, pp 46–9, 346–8


### Questions

a What does this extract tell you about Peter's attitude towards the role of a monarch?

* b Why was Alexis a focus for those forces of tradition hostile to his father, Peter?

* c 'The two factors essential in governing, namely, order and defence' (lines 8–9). Did Peter's reforms stem from his readiness to fight his country's traditional enemies?

* d 'I will cut you off . . . like a gangrenous growth' (lines 16–17). What did happen to Alexis?

# 6 A Contemporary Assessment of Peter

Such were his merits that all true sons of Russia wished him to be immortal; while his age and solid constitution gave everyone the expectation of seeing him alive for many more years; he has ended his life — o, horrible wound! — at a time when he was just beginning to live
5   after many labours, troubles, sorrows, calamities, and perils of death. Do not we see well enough how much we have angered Thee, O Lord, and abused Thine patience! . . .

He was your Samson, Russia. . . . Finding an army that was disorderly at home, weak in the field, the butt of the enemy's derision, he
10   created one that was useful to the fatherland, terrible to the enemy, renowned and glorious everywhere. In defending his fatherland he at the same time returned to it lands that had been wrested from it and augmented it by the acquisition of new provinces. . . .

Russia, he was your first Japhet! He has accomplished a deed heretofore
15   unheard of in Russia: the building and sailing of ships . . . and it opened up to thee, Russia, the way to all corners of the earth, and carried thine power and glory to the remotest oceans, to the very limits set by thy own interests and by justice. . . .

He was your Moses, O Russia! For are not his laws like the strong visor
20   of justice and the unbreakable fetters of crime! And do not his clear regulations illuminate your path, most high governing Senate, and that of all principal and particular administrations established by him! . . .

O Russia, he was your Solomon. . . . This is proven by the manifold philosophic disciplines introduced by him and by his showing and
25   imparting to many of his subjects the knowledge of a variety of inventions and crafts unknown to us before his time. To this also bear witness the ranks and titles, the civil laws, the rules of social intercourse, propitious customs, and codes of behaviour, and also the improvement of our external appearance. . . .

30   And he was your David and your Constantine, O Russian Church! . . . What a zeal he has displayed in combatting superstition, adulatory hypocrisy, and the senseless, inimical, ruinous schism nesting in our midst. . . .

Most distinguished man! Can a short oration encompass his im-
35   measurable glory? . . . He has gone — but he has not left us poor and wretched: his enormous power and glory — manifested in the deeds I spoke of before — have remained with us. As he has shaped his Russia, so she will remain: he has made her lovable to good men, and she will be loved; he has made her fearful to her enemies, and she will be feared; he
40   has glorified her throughout the world, and her glory will not end. He has left us spiritual, civil, and military reforms. For if his perishable body has left us, his spirit remains.

> 'A Funeral Oration For The Most Illustrious And Most Sovereign Emperor And Autocrat Of All Russia, Peter The Great', F. Prokopovich, 8 March 1725, trans. by M. Raeff, *Peter the Great: Reformer or Revolutionary?*, D. C. Heath, 1963, pp 76–8

## Questions

    *a*  In what ways does this illustrate 'the uncritical admiration and sense of awe which the collaborators and disciples of Peter displayed' (Raeff)?

\*  *b*  'He was your Samson . . . your first Japhet' (lines 8—18). What changes did Peter make in the Russian army and navy, and what were the new provinces acquired as a result?

\*  *c*  'The reform of the administration is the most striking aspect of his work '(Klyuchevsky). Was Peter really the 'Moses' (lines 19—22) of Russia?

\*  *d*  How did Peter tackle 'the senseless, inimical, ruinous schism nesting in our midst' (lines 32—3)?

\*  *e*  Did Peter achieve anything by trying to alter 'the rules of social intercourse . . . the improvement of our external appearance' (lines 27—9)?

\*  *f*  'As he has shaped his Russia, so she will remain . . . his spirit remains' (lines 37–42). Did this prophecy become fact?


## 7  Historical Assessments of Peter

(a) A number of events . . . served simultaneously to bring Muscovy closer to the West. . . . The Time of Troubles . . . underlined Russia's military backwardness . . . [and] the need for armies equipped and trained on western lines. Military needs were to set the tone of
5  'borrowing' for the century. . . . The mid-century schism in the Russian Orthodox Church . . . obliged the authorities to use the services of theologians, translators and teachers from the clergy of Muscovy's better educated Orthodox neighbours, notably the Ukraine and Byelorussia. . . . The annexation of the previously Polish ruled left-bank
10  Ukraine to Muscovy in 1654. . . . [also] formed an important element in seventeenth-century Westernization.

    It is against this general background, in a century which also saw intensified diplomatic ties with most Western states, that one notes a steady flow of foreign personnel into Muscovy. . . . Some of them
15  served the tsars as special agents, travelling abroad to recruit mercenaries and craftsmen, while others were licensed to set up manufactures, such as the Dutchman Andrew Vinius' Tula ironworks (1632), Johann van Sveden's Moscow paper mills (1660s). . . . and the textile mills set up by Paullson and Tabert in the 1680s. . . . In 1679 Jacob Reutenfels, an
20  envoy for Tuscany, remarked on the rising standards of Muscovite workmanship, which were achieved 'thanks to their dealings with foreigners, which become freer with every day'. . . . By the middle of the century the Moscow Armoury comprised a complex of workshops producing not only small arms but also a wide range of useful and
25  decorative objects for the royal household. It has been described as a

seventeenth-century 'Academy of Arts'. . . . It is [also] possible to trace new devices in art and architecture to foreign graphic material. . . . Western innovations were adopted or perceived only by a small elite, confined to court, government and church circles, yet this
30 does not detract from their significance. . . . Peter's reforms were not such a revolutionary break with an uneducated and inward-looking past as has sometimes been suggested.

L. A. J. Hughes, *The Seventeenth-Century 'Renaissance' in Russia*, in *History Today*, Vol. 30, 1980, pp 42—5

(b) It is now a truism to say that the view of Peter's reign as . . . a very sharp transition from darkness to light, from barbarism to civilisation, is
35 untenable. . . . It tended to gloss over or ignore the failures against the Turks, in Central Asia and, in the long run, against Persia, which had to be set against the great success won in Europe. It grossly underestimated the scope and effect of the changes in Russian life which were already under way long before Peter was born. Its view of the Russian people as
40 sunk, until his advent, in depths of ignorance and superstition from which only his daemonic energy and unbending will could raise them, was unfair in view of the progress made before his reign had begun. Even more objectionable and unrealistic was the assumption that Russia had scarcely existed in any meaningful sense before it was discovered and
45 influenced by Europe. Within a generation of Peter's death this had begun to be recognised and resented by some patriotic Russians. 'Those who proclaim that we were nothing but barbarians before Peter the Great . . . do not know what they are saying,' protested the poet Sumarokov, 'our ancestors were in no way inferior to us'. . . .
50 The uncritically admiring attitude to Peter so common by the end of his reign also ignored the extent to which his work was incomplete at his death and the obstacles which it encountered in the mere geography, physical and human, of Russia. In a huge and thinly populated country with very poor communications, the relations of much of the population
55 with the government were at best slight and intermittent. Ambitious innovating legislation was harder to enforce effectively than anywhere else in Europe; and the fact that so many of Peter's decrees were highly detailed and specific in their provisions merely accentuated the gulf between what the monarch ordered and what actually happened (or
60 more often failed to happen) in some distant province. More important, the tsar's admirers ignored the fact that the results of much of his work were destructive rather than constructive. . . . Peter's insistence that the ruling class should adopt western dress and to some extent western customs, and even so far as possible receive a western-type education, had
65 far-reaching implications. It meant that the division between lord and peasant, between rulers and ruled, between well-to-do and poor, was now more clearcut, more visible and more difficult to bridge. . . . The great administrative reforms of the reign had, on a different level, some of the same results. By increasing the number of officials in Russia and

70  making them cogs in an increasingly elaborate machine Peter
    undermined, indeed destroyed, the essentially personal character of
    authority which had been characteristic of Muscovite Russia. . . .
       Few of the objectives for which he strove so hard and long were new.
    Almost without exception they were inherent in the history and
75  geographical position of Russia and the necessities which these created.
    Greater military strength; a Baltic coastline; a more developed economic
    life: none of these was a new ambition. None was inspired by an irruption
    of novel ideas or foreign influences. All, and especially the first two, had a
    solid Muscovite tradition behind them, while even the transformation of
80  Church-state relations completed by 1721 had been foreshadowed to
    some extent by the great conflicts of the 1650s and 1660s. The navy was
    indeed a novelty; but though it was, together with the building of St.
    Petersburg, the most personal of all Peter's major creations and the one
    with least foothold in Muscovite tradition, it was also the least important.
85  In the structure and workings of Russian society great changes were
    made. Yet this was done by accelerating developments already under
    way as much as by introducing anything really new. . . .
       Russia under Peter the Great can thus be regarded as undergoing, in the
    main, a process of forced and greatly accelerated evolution rather than of
90  true revolution. Peter lacked almost completely the intellectual equip-
    ment of a modern revolutionary. He had no ideology, no articulated
    system of general ideas to guide his actions, no clear vision of a march of
    history irresistibly impelling Russia in a particular direction.
       M. S. Anderson, *Peter the Great*, Thames and Hudson, 1978, pp
    170—4

*Questions*

a  How do these views of the importance of Peter compare with the
   contemporary views found in extracts 4 and 6?
* b  In the light of these two extracts, is it true that the view of the Russian
   people as being sunk 'in depths of ignorance' is unfair 'in view of the
   progress made before his reign had begun' (lines 39—42) Did Peter
   merely 'accelerate developments already under way' (lines 86–7)?
c  What reasons does Anderson give for believing Peter's work to be
   incomplete?
* d  Is it fair to say that much of Peter's work was 'destructive rather than
   constructive' (line 62)?
* e  Did Peter have 'no clear vision' (line 92) of where he was taking
   Russia?

# X    The 'General Crisis' Controversy

## Introduction

In 1643 the preacher Jeremiah Whittaker told the English House of Commons that they did not stand alone in rebellion: 'These are days of shaking and the shaking is universal.' Contemporaries echoed this view. The French historian Robert Mentet de Salmonet wrote in 1649 that the century would become famous for 'the great and strange revolutions that have happen'd in it'. Indeed it was a century of major wars, political and social revolts, and vital economic change. Voltaire, reviewing it in 1756, commented that the century witnessed a 'general crisis', thus foreshadowing the lively debate that has taken place in the twentieth century.

In 1935 Paul Hazard argued that the seventeenth century saw a major intellectual crisis in his *La Crise de la conscience européene*. R. B. Merriman extended this concept of 'crisis' to both the political and economic fields by comparing six European upheavals in the 1640s (in England, France, Catalonia, Naples, Portugal, and Holland) in his *Six Contemporaneous Revolutions* (Oxford, 1938). Other historians were quick to point out revolts elsewhere, not only in Europe but throughout the world, and R. Mousnier concluded in his *Les XVIe et XVIIe Siècles* (Paris, 1954) that the seventeenth century was 'a time of crisis which affected all Mankind' with manifestations in the demographic, political, economic, social, and intellectual spheres.

The nature and origin of this 'crisis' was soon hotly debated. Some argued a basic climatic change (extract 1), and many saw the crisis as primarily an economic one. In 1954 E. J. Hobsbawm put forward the argument that the seventeenth century marked the transformation from a 'feudal' to a 'capitalistic' society in his 'The Crisis of the Seventeenth Century' (extract 2). This led to many articles on the subject in the journal *Past and Present*. Some historians rejected the rather Marxist approach of Hobsbawm (extract 3) and, more recently, some have even denied that there was any major economic crisis (extract 4) because the evidence is not by any means conclusive. H. R. Trevor-Roper argued in his 'The General Crisis of the Seventeenth Century' that the crisis was not economic but a crisis in the relation of the state to society, a conflict between a puritanically minded opposition (the 'country') and a parasitic bureaucracy (the 'court') (extract 5). This view has been under heavy attack, both for being too heavily based on events in England rather than

Europe as a whole, and for underestimating important factors, such as the impact of war (extract 6) and the increasing demands of absolutism, especially in the field of taxation (extract 7). T. K. Rabb argues that the immense changes in the sixteenth century had produced a world where 'The old answers no longer work, whether in religion or in studies of nature' and 'new ones have still to be found', and he sees the seventeenth-century 'crisis' as being a search for certainty.

Doubts about the validity of applying the word 'crisis' to an entire century have been expressed by some historians. J. H. Elliott in his 'Revolution and Continuity in Early Modern Europe' pointed out that there were just as many revolts in the 1560s as in the 1640s, but no one has argued the case for a 'general crisis' of the sixteenth century. He feels it is the combination of political with economic crisis that has led to the acceptance of the view, although the evidence for the economic crisis is not conclusive and the relationship between economic crisis and political revolution far from straightforward. He argues that much of the so-called 'crisis' is the product of hindsight: historians looking at the revolts in the light of later events (extract 8).

The debate is still very much alive and there is no doubt that it does raise many questions that are worthy of discussion, not only about the seventeenth century, but also about historical methods and approach.

## Further Reading

A selection of articles are published in T. Aston, *Crisis in Europe 1560–1660*, Routledge & Kegan Paul, 1965, and G.Parker and L. M. Smith, *The General Crisis of the Seventeenth Century*, Routledge & Kegan Paul, 1978. The 'general crisis' is discussed in the context of the Thirty Years War in J. V. Polisensky, *The Thirty Years War*, Batsford, 1971. Also recommended is T. K. Rabb, *The Struggle for Stability in Early Modern Europe*, Oxford University Press, 1976.

# I    A Climatic Crisis

The notebooks of the leading astronomers of the later seventeenth century . . . all record the almost complete absence of sunspots between about 1645 and 1715. . . . There was also a failure to observe either aurora borealis (northern lights) or a corona during solar eclipses during
5    this period. These data cannot be dismissed as absence of evidence; they constitute genuine evidence of absence, and they are supported by other facts. First, the detailed drawings of the early astronomers – some of them daily compilations – reveal the sun rotating in a significantly different way in the mid-seventeenth century. Second, measurements of
10    the radioactive isotope of carbon, carbon-14 (C), deposited in past centuries reveals a notable aberration between 1650 and 1750: there was an enormous increase in C deposits, indicating an abundance of carbon in

the earth's atmosphere, a circumstance normally associated with a
reduction in solar energy . . . and an overall decline in solar energy
15 would explain such disparate yet related facts as the advance of glaciers all
over the world; the late ripening of grapes in the French vineyards; the
late flowering of the imperial cherry trees in imperial Japan . . . all point
to a cooler climate, and in particular to cooler and wetter summers, across
the globe in the mid-seventeenth century. In a world dependent largely
20 on vegetable and cereal crops, such changes could not fail to be
serious. . . .

A fall of one degree C in overall temperatures – and that is the magnitude of the change during the 'Little Ice Age' – restricts the growing
season for plants by three or four weeks and reduces the maximum
25 altitude for cultivation by about 500 feet. The expansion of population in
the sixteenth century had led to the cultivation of many marginal
highlands; a colder summer would reduce or perhaps remove the yield of
such areas, leaving their populations on the threshold of starvation.
Diminished food reserves, producing (effectively) serious over-
30 population, presented a favourable terrain for the spread of diseases. . . .

There was no real escape from this dilemma, which economists would
term a 'high-level equilibrium trap': the inputs and outputs of the
agricultural system had reached a balance that could be broken only by
heavy capital investment and new technology. This European agriculture
35 could not provide . . . yield ratios remained stable and even
fell. . . . And, wherever improved yields were achieved, whether
through better methods or increased area of cultivation, the surplus was
soon swallowed up by the growing population: there was little capital
accumulation, therefore little land improvement or technical innovation,
40 and therefore little increase in the supply of daily bread. There were only
three choices facing a population caught in this trap: migration, death or
revolt.

G. Parker and L. M. Smith, *The General Crisis of the Seventeenth
Century*, Routledge and Kegan Paul, 1978, pp 6–9

## Questions

*a* State, in your own words, the argument for there having been a
climatic change in the seventeenth century.

*b* What effects would such a climatic change produce? Do you think
these would have been sufficient to account for a 'general crisis'?

*c* What is the significance of (i) sunspots (line 2), (ii) a corona during a
solar eclipse (line 4) and (iii) measuring the radioactive isotope of
carbon (lines 9–10)?

*d* What do economists mean by a 'high-level equilibrium trap' (line
32)?

\* *e* What evidence is there that the majority of people in the seventeenth century had to choose between 'migration, death, or revolt'
(lines 41–2)?

* *ƒ* Scientists and historians are 'engaged in different branches of the *same* study: the study of man and his environment' (E. H. Carr). What does science have to offer the historian?

## 2 From Feudalism to Capitalism: The Argument For

There can be little doubt that the sixteenth century came nearer to creating the conditions for a really widespread adoption of the capitalist mode of production than any previous age; perhaps because of the impetus given by overseas loot, perhaps because of the encouragement of
5 rapidly growing population and markets and rising prices. . . . Yet the expansion bred its own obstacles. We may briefly consider some of them.

Except perhaps in England no 'agrarian revolution' of a capitalist type accompanied industrial change, as it was to do in the eighteenth century; though there was plenty of upheaval in the countryside. Here again we
10 find the generally feudal nature of the social framework distorting and diverting forces which might otherwise have made for a direct advance towards modern capitalism. . . . It is improbable that there was much technical innovation . . . and certain that the increase in agrarian output did not keep pace with demand. Hence towards the end of the period
15 there are signs of diminishing returns and food-shortage, of exporting areas using up their crops for local needs, etc., preludes to the famines and epidemics of the crisis-period. . . . The rural population, subject to the double pressure of landlords and townsmen (not to mention the State), and in any case much less capable of protecting itself against famine and
20 war than they, suffered. In some regions this shortsighted 'squeeze' may actually have led to a declining trend in productivity during the seventeenth century. The countryside was sacrificed to lord, town and State. . . .

What happened in the non-agricultural sectors depended largely
25 on the agricultural. Costs of manufacture may have been unduly raised by the more rapid rise of agrarian than of industrial prices, thus narrowing the profit-margin of the manufacturers. . . . The rural market as a whole must have proved disappointing . . . a middle and rich peasantry is about as uninviting a market for mass manufactures as may be
30 found, and does not encourage capitalists to revolutionise production. Its wants are traditional; most of its wealth goes into more land and cattle, or into hoards, or into new building, or even into sheer waste. . . . An additional factor increased the difficulties of manufacture: the rise in labour costs. For there is evidence that – in the towns at least – the
35 bargaining power of labour rose sharply during the crisis, perhaps owing to the fall or stagnation in town populations. . . . Moreover, the slackening of population increase and the stabilisation of prices must have depressed manufacturers further.

These different aspects of the crisis may be reduced to a single formula:
40 economic expansion took place within a social framework which it was not yet strong enough to burst, and in ways adapted to it rather than to

the world of modern capitalism. Specialists in the Jacobean period must
determine what actually precipitated the crisis: the decline in American
silver, the collapse of the Baltic market or some of many other possible
45  factors. Once the first crack appeared, the whole unstable structure was
bound to totter. It did totter, and in the subsequent period of economic
crisis and social upheaval the decisive shift from capitalist enterprise
adapted to a generally feudal framework to capitalist enterprise transforming the world in its own pattern, took place. The Revolution in
50  England was thus the most dramatic incident in the crisis, and its turning-
point. 'This nation', wrote Samuel Fortrey in 1663 in his *England's Interest
and Improvement*, 'can expect no less than to become the most great and
flourishing of all others'. It could and it did; and the effects on the world
were to be portentous.

E. J. Hobsbawm, 'The Crisis of the Seventeenth Century' in *Past
and Present*, no 5, 1954, pp 46—9

## Questions

a   Why does Hobsbawm believe the seventeenth century marked an
economic crisis? What kind of economic crisis does he depict?
b   What is the 'capitalist mode of production' (lines 2—3)?
c   What does Hobsbawm mean by the 'feudal nature of the social
framework' (line 10)?
d   Why did changes in the non-agricultural sector depend largely on
changes in the agricultural sector (lines 24—5)?
*  e   What is the distinction between a 'capitalist enterprise adapted to a
generally feudal framework' and a 'capitalist enterprise transforming
the world in its own pattern' (lines 47—9), and why, in this context,
was 'the Revolution in England' the turning-point?
f   Is a climatic crisis irrelevant to Hobsbawm's argument?

## 3  From Feudalism to Capitalism: The Argument Against

According to the Marxists, and to some other historians . . . the crisis of
the seventeenth century was at bottom a crisis of production, and the
motive force behind at least some of the revolutions was the force of
the producing *bourgeoisie*, hampered in their economic activity by the
5  obsolete, wasteful, restrictive, but jealously defended productive system
of 'feudal' society. According to this view, the crisis of production was
general in Europe, but it was only in England that the forces of
'capitalism', thanks to their greater development and their representation
in parliament, were able to triumph. . . .
10      This Marxist thesis has been advanced by many able writers, but, in
spite of their arguments, I do not believe that it has been proved or even

that any solid evidence has been adduced to sustain it. It is of course easy to
show that there were economic changes in the seventeenth century, and
that, at least in England, industrial capitalism was more developed in 1700
than in 1600; but to do this is not the same as to show either that the
economic changes precipitated the revolutions in Europe, or that English
capitalism was directly forwarded by the Puritan 'victory' of 1640–
1660. These are hypotheses, which may of course be true; but it is equally
possible that they are untrue: that problems of production were irrelevant
to the seventeenth-century revolutions generally, and that English
capitalist development was independent of the Puritan revolution in the
sense that it would or could have occurred without that revolution,
perhaps even was retarded or interrupted by it. If it is to be shown that the
English Puritan revolution was a successful 'bourgeois revolution' . . . it
must be shown either that the men who made the revolution aimed at
such a result, or that those who wished for such a result forwarded the
revolution, or that such a result would not have been attained
without the revolution. . . . Now in fact no advocate of the Marxist
theory seems to me to have established any of these necessary links in the
argument. . . .

Altogether it seems to me that the Marxist identification of the
seventeenth-century revolutions with 'bourgeois' 'capitalist' revolutions,
successful in England, unsuccessful elsewhere, is a mere *a priori*
hypothesis. The Marxists see, as we all see, that, at some time between the
discovery of America and the Industrial Revolution, the basis was laid for
a new 'capitalist' form of society. Believing, as a matter of doctrine, that
such a change cannot be achieved peacefully but requires a violent 'break-
through' of a new class, a 'bourgeois revolution', they look for such a
revolution. Moreover, seeing that the country which led in this process
was England, they look for such a revolution in England. And when they
find, exactly half-way between these terminal dates, the violent Puritan
revolution in England, they cry εὕρηκα ! Thereupon the other European
revolutions fall easily into place as abortive bourgeois revolutions. The
hypothesis, once stated, is illustrated by other hypotheses. It has yet to
be proved by evidence. And it may be that it rests on entirely false
premises.

H. R. Trevor-Roper, 'The General Crisis of the Seventeenth
Century', in *Past and Present* No 16, 1959, pp 35–7

## Questions

* *a*  What is the Marxist interpretation of history?
  *b*  Does Trevor-Roper's summary of the Marxist view of 'the crisis'
       (lines 1–9) apply to extract 2?
  *c*  Why does Trevor-Roper believe the Marxists have not provided
       evidence for their views? Do you think his criticisms are justified?
* *d*  Is there any evidence that the unrest in Europe in the 1640s was the
       product of bourgeois revolutions?

* *e*   Trevor-Roper implies that Marxist bias has resulted in a distorted
view of the seventeenth century, but to what extent can any historian
be objective?

## 4   How Great was the Economic Crisis?

For I should like to issue a few notes of warning here. Firstly, seventeenth-
century slumps are too often judged against the background of a really
spectacular boom at the end of the sixteenth century. This was not a
normal expansion but something exceptional even for those times of
5   violent fluctuation. Second, I doubt whether so much faith and reliance
on price statistics themselves is justified. They reflect after all only a
restricted aspect of economic activity, and there is a tendency to attach
disproportionate value to them because they are actually the only statistic
data we possess for many countries over an extensive period in past
10   centuries. . . . Third, national and regional variations, even in price
statistics, are much greater than some historians are willing to admit. . . .
In times of general slump years of recovery and improvement can still be
very important. . . .

As compared with the price revolution of the sixteenth century, of
15   which there were offshoots right into the first decades of the seventeenth
century, the time that followed shows up very favourably. There is a
certain global stabilisation that must have had favourable influence on
wages. . . . I should prefer to qualify the fall in the import of silver from
Spanish America as a stabilising factor for the economy, which had been
20   ravaged by an all-too-extravagant inflation. I admit at once that the
circulation of money was here and there probably slowed down,
hampering economic growth, but it seems to me wrong to jump to the
conclusion that the total supply of currency was reduced to a minimum.
Hoarding and export of precious metals, the latter especially to Asia, did
25   indeed drain money from circulation, but there was always a new supply,
especially later on in the seventeenth century, e.g. gold from Brazil; and
in the meantime copper met the emergency. Now if we consider
conditions in France in the seventeenth century and then calculate the
supply of gold and silver (in coinage) together with that of the country's
30   imports, we shall probably find more money in circulation than in the
sixteenth century. Finally, I think we meet the same picture in the general
situation of the population. I admit we know very little about
seventeenth-century population growth, but from existing data I get the
impression of a slight rise rather than of a spectacular drop. . . .
35   Certainly an enormous shift took place in seventeenth-century
Europe. . . . The whole weight of commerce and industry moved away
from the countries around the Mediterranean, especially Italy and Spain,
to the Atlantic coast, to western France, England and the Low Countries
in particular. At the same time the balance, assisted partly by the
40   destructive Thirty Years' War, shifted from south and central Germany

to the North Sea ports of Hamburg and Bremen and from Poland and the
Baltic coast to Scandinavia. . . . If this shift is to be called a 'crisis', I have
no objection, but it is not unrelieved gloom. Within a process of general
stabilisation there was a shifting of gravity which brought new countries
45   new profits.
        I. Schoffer, 'Did Holland's Golden Age Coincide with a Period of
        Crisis?', in *Bijdragen en Mededelingen van het Historisch
        Genootschap*, LXXVIII, 1964, reprinted in G. Parker and L. M.
        Smith, *The General Crisis of the Seventeenth Century*, Routledge
        and Kegan Paul, 1978, pp 95–8

## Questions

*a*   Why does Schoffer feel that the evidence of (i) price statistics (line 6),
      (ii) money circulation (line 21) and (iii) population figures (lines 31–
      4) is not great enough to indicate any great economic crisis?
\*   *b*   Is there any other evidence available to a historian wishing to assess the
      economic climate of the seventeenth century?
\*   *c*   What was the 'price revolution of the sixteenth century' (line 14), and
      what effects did it have on the seventeenth century?
*d*   What economic 'shift' (line 35) took place in the seventeenth century?
      Did this constitute a crisis?
*e*   In the light of the first four extracts, would you argue that the unrest in
      the seventeenth century was primarily economic?

## 5   A Crisis of the State

Every officer, at every court, in every country, lived by the same system.
He was paid a trivial 'fee' or salary and, for the rest, made what he could in
the field which his office had opened to him . . . it was taken for granted
that he would charge a reasonable sum for audiences, favours, signatures,
5   that he would exploit his office to make good bargains, that he would
invest public money, while in his hands, on his own account. . . . Thus
each old office granted, each new office created, meant a new burden on
the subject. . . .
        All bureaucracies tend to expand . . . But whereas today such
10   inflation is curbed by the needs of the Treasury, in the sixteenth century
the needs of the Treasury positively encouraged it. For offices . . . were
not granted freely: they were sold, and – at least in the beginning – the
purchase-price went to the Crown. If the Crown could sell more and
more offices at higher and higher prices, leaving the 'officers' to be paid
15   by the country, this was an indirect, if also a cumbrous and exasperating
way of taxing the country. . . . [This] could only be borne if society itself
was expanding in wealth and numbers. . . . Already, by 1590, the cracks
are beginning to appear. The strains of the last years of Philip II's wars
release everywhere a growing volume of complaint: complaint which is

20  not directed against constitutional faults—against the despotism of kings
or the claims of the Estates — but against this or that aspect or consequence
of the growth and cost of a parasitic bureaucracy. For, of course, although
war has not created the problem, war aggravates it: the more the costs of
government are raised, the more the government resorts to those now
25  traditional financial expedients: creation and sale of new offices, sale or
long lease, at undervalues, of Crown or Church lands, creation of
monopolies, raising of 'feudal' taxes. . . .
    [By the 1620s] a new attitude of mind had been created. . . . It was an
attitude of hatred: hatred of 'the court' and its courtiers, hatred of princely
30  follies and bureaucratic corruption, hatred of the Renaissance itself: in
short, puritanism. . . .
    There were also differences in society. . . . For instance, in England
the cost of the court fell most heavily on the gentry: they were the tax-
paying class . . . [but] in France the *noblesse* were exempt from taxation,
35  and the *taille* and *gabelle*, which were multiplied by the early Bourbons,
fell heaviest on the peasants. . . . In England, when revolution came, it
was a great revolution, led and controlled by the gentry; in France, there
were . . . revolts—little but serious revolts—of the peasants. Nevertheless, if the rebels were different, the general grievance against which they
40  rebelled—the character and cost of the state—was the same. . . . From
1620 to 1640 this is the cry of the country, the problem of the court . . .
and these demands, these problems are not constitutional, they are not
concerned with monarchy or republic, Crown or Parliament. Nor are
they economic: they are not concerned with methods of production.
45  Essentially they are demands for emancipation from the burden of
centralisation; for reduction of fees; reduction of useless, expensive
offices, including—even in Spain—clerical offices; abolition of the sale of
offices . . . [and] abolition of hereditary offices. . . .
    Such, as it seems to me, was the 'general crisis of the seventeenth
50  century'. It was a crisis not of the constitution nor of the system of
production, but of the state, or rather, of the relation of the state to
society.
            H. R. Trevor-Roper, 'The General Crisis of the Seventeenth
            Century', in *Past and Present* no 16, 1959, pp 44−8, 50−1, 61

## Questions

a  Why does Trevor-Roper believe the seventeenth century witnessed a
   crisis in the relation between state and society (lines 49−52)?
b  What reasons does he give for calling the bureaucracy 'parasitic' (line
   22)?
c  What does Trevor-Roper mean by the term 'the court' (line 29)?
*  d  Was 'the character and cost of the state' (line 40) the 'general
      grievance' (line 39) that lay behind both the English Civil War and the
      French Fronde?
*  e  From your knowledge of events in any one European country, do you

believe Trevor-Roper's ideas are applicable to the disturbances that took place in the mid seventeenth century?

*f* Does the argument that there was an economic crisis have any bearing on Trevor-Roper's belief that the 'court' was too costly?

## 6 The Importance of War

To say simply that '*war aggravates*' the problem of the growth of a parasitic bureaucracy is surely rather a remarkable understatement. Admittedly, '*the sixteenth-century wars had led to no such revolutions*' but they had bequeathed a terrible inheritance to the seventeenth century;
5 and, on top of this, seventeenth-century wars were fought on a very different scale. . . . This new scale of warfare created problems of an entirely new magnitude and order for the rulers of seventeenth-century states. It placed an additional enormous burden on economies already subjected to heavy strain . . . it also meant extending the power of the
10 King over his subjects, in order to draw on the resources of provinces and of social classes hitherto undertaxed or exempt. . . . The essential clue to the revolutionary situation of the 1640s is, I suspect, to be found in the determination of governments to exercise fuller control over their states without yet having the administrative means or fiscal resources to ensure
15 obedience to their will; and that determination sprang in the first instance from something which could not be gainsaid and brooked no delay — the imperious demands of war.

> J. H. Elliott, 'Trevor-Roper's 'General Crisis' Symposium', in
> *Past and Present* no 18, 1960, pp 29—30

### Questions

*a* What is Elliott's criticism of Trevor-Roper's ideas?
* *b* What 'terrible inheritance' (line 4) did sixteenth-century wars leave Europe?
* *c* Why were seventeenth-century wars fought on a 'very different scale' (lines 5—6), and what changes in the methods of warfare took place?
*d* State, in your own words, the reasons Elliott gives for the unrest in Europe.
*e* What were 'the imperious demands of war' (line 17) on a state? (See also the next extract.)

## 7 The Role of Absolutism

The pair of concepts, court—country, has scarcely any European validity. . . . The revolts were by no means directed against a stagnating parasitism, but against a dynamic absolutism which, with its taxation policy, violated the customary laws and threatened to disrupt the social
5 balance or deprive parts of the population of their livelihood. In

Catalonia and Portugal the revolts were precipitated not by dissatisfaction with the established order, but by dissatisfaction with Olivares's attempt to alter the established order when he demanded that the viceroyalties should contribute towards the costs of Spain's foreign policy
10 side by side with Castille. The revolt in Naples followed after a number of years of large contributions to the Spanish war chest, which not only had been economically devastating, but also had created chaos in the traditional distribution of authority and wealth. The revolt in Palermo took place under the slogan, 'Long live the King and down with taxes', a
15 slogan that is to be found time and time again during the revolts of the French peasants. The opposition of the Parlement of Paris in the 1640s had no ideological aim, but was concentrated against the Crown's fiscal legislation; and the Fronde of the Parlement was triggered by a legislation that would have decreased the Parlement's own privileges. In England
20 the trends are less clear, but even in this case there is an apparent conflict between the monarchy's attempt to strengthen its economic independence and the taxpayer's defence of his customary rights. Even in the *coup d'état* in the Netherlands the fiscal element is present, though in this case the conflict was precipitated by the states of the province of Holland
25 refusing to continue payment of the soliders they had to maintain, which were under the command of the Stadtholder.

The common factor in the contemporaneous revolutions is thus something far less subtle than Trevor-Roper's dualism between court and country. We do not need to look for abstract similarities between the
30 social structures of the societies in revolt, for there is a concrete similarity between the policy of the governments concerned, that is their attempts to increase their income or to secure control over the state revenue regardless of customary rights. . . . Behind the conflict we find the same thing everywhere: the State's demand for higher revenues. In some cases
35 the tax demands were coupled with financial reforms that were not necessarily unfair, but which undermined customary rights; in other cases the increased burden of taxation came to rest on the population groups already living below the bread line. . . . [Thus] the tax demands disrupted the social balance. They did not create a revolutionary
40 situation: they were in themselves a revolution. The six contemporaneous revolutions can only be seen as one if we rechristen them 'the six contemporaneous reactions'. . . . The problem of the crisis is therefore the problem of absolutism.

N. Steensgaard, 'Det syttende Arhundredes Krise', in *Historisk Tidsskrift* (Dansk) XII, 1970, trans. by Paula Hostrup-Jessen in G. Parker and L. M. Smith, *The General Crisis of the Seventeenth Century*, Routledge and Kegan Paul, 1978, pp 42–4

## Questions

*a* Why does Steensgaard reject Trevor-Roper's court–country concept as having no European validity?

*b* What evidence does he offer that 'the State's demand for higher revenues' (line 34) was the basic cause of unrest, and why would he therefore rechristen the revolts 'contemporaneous reactions' (line 42)?

*c* What do you think Steensgaard means by concluding that the 'problem of the crisis is therefore the problem of absolutism' (lines 42–3)?

*d* How effective do you find Steensgaard's arguments?

*e* Having read the last three extracts, do you feel that any of the theories throw valuable light on the nature of the unrest in Europe, and justify talk of a 'general crisis'?


# 8 The Problem of Hindsight

Between us and Early Modern Europe lies the late eighteenth century, dominated for us by two events which seem to have done more than anything else to shape our own civilisation – the French Revolution and the Industrial Revolution in England. During the nineteenth century,
5   each of these became a paradigm – an exemplar, in one instance, for political and social development, and in the other for economic development. . . . Consciously or unconsciously, nineteenth- and twentieth-century historians have looked at revolts in Early Modern Europe in the light of the late eighteenth-century revolutions, and of their
10   assessment of them. This has frequently provided them with valuable insights into the origins of great events; but the very fact that they applied to many of these Early Modern revolts the word 'revolution' suggests the possibility of unconscious distortions, which may itself give us some cause for unease. . . .
15       Perhaps our principal expectation of a revolutionary ideology is that it should break with the past and aspire to establish a new social order. . . . Early Modern European society was dominated by the idea not of progress, but of a return to a golden age in the past. . . . How far can historians accustomed to look for *innovation* among revolutionaries, enter
20   into the minds of men who themselves were obsessed by *renovation* – by the desire to return to old customs and privileges, and to an old order of society?. . . The sixteenth and seventeenth centuries did indeed see significant changes in the texture of European life, but these changes occurred inside the resilient framework of the aristocratic–monarchical
25   state. . . . Renovation in theory, does not of itself preclude innovation in practice; and the deliberate attempt to return to old ways may lead men, in spite of themselves, into startlingly new departures. There remained, too, sufficient room for the ruling class to be able to challenge the State at the two points were its activities were most likely to influence the
30   character of national life. By resisting the state in the matter of taxation, it might destroy, or prevent the establishment of, a major obstacle to economic development; and by resisting its claims to enforce religious

uniformity, it might remove a major obstacle to intellectual advance. If
significant change came to certain European societies in the sixteenth and
35   seventeenth centuries, it came because this challenge was effectively
carried through.

By the eighteenth century, the growing awareness of man's capacity to
control and improve his environment would make it more fashionable
than it had been in the seventeenth century to think in terms of
40   innovation. . . . Until then, revolts continued to be played out within
the context of the ambitions of the State on the one hand, and the
determination of the dominant social groups to preserve their heritage,
on the other.

J. H. Elliott, 'Revolution and Continuity in Early Modern
Europe', in *Past and Present* no 42, 1969, pp 40, 43−4, 55−6

## Questions

a   What was the nature of political change in the seventeenth century
according to Elliott?

b   What distinction is there between 'revolt' and 'revolution'?

*  c   Why are the French Revolution and the Industrial Revolution seen as
a 'paradigm' (i.e. a model example) 'for political and social development and . . . for economic development' (lines 5−7)? Is Elliott right
in thinking this has affected our view of the seventeenth century?

*  d   A crisis is 'a state of affairs in which a decisive change for better or
worse is imminent' (*Shorter Oxford Dictionary*). Can you apply the
word 'crisis' to an entire century, and, if you can, what 'decisive
change' took place in the seventeenth century?

*  e   'There was an economic and political crisis all over western and
central Europe in the seventeenth century' (C. Hill). Would you
agree? Or is the 'general crisis' theory just a product of historians
wishing to give the century in between the Renaissance and the
Enlightenment an identity of its own?